SHAKEN.
NOT
BROKEN.

SURVIVING THE QUAKE WITHIN & WITHOUT

NAMRATA KOHLI

ISBN
Hardcase 979-8-89475-995-1
Paperback 979-8-89446-659-0

Dedication

To my family,

For your boundless love and support, for being my constant source of encouragement every step of the way, and for nurturing the storyteller within me. Thank you for believing in my dreams, for standing by me through every trial, and for filling my life with inspiration.

To my husband, Gautam,

For being my rock, keeping me grounded, and bringing us both out of Taroko National Park alive. For being my therapist-at-home, listening to all my crazy ideas, reading every chapter of this memoir as I penned it, and always giving me the single word of feedback I needed: "Good." Thank you for being the calm in my storm, the peace in my anxiety, and my always happy place.

This memoir is as much yours as it is mine.

Contents

Introduction

On 3 April 2024, Taiwan experienced its worst earthquake in a quarter of a century.[1] It was a 7.4 magnitude earthquake with an epicentre 10 km from Hualien, near the east coast of Taiwan. The worst impact of this earthquake was seen in Taroko National Park, a UNESCO World Heritage site renowned for its towering mountains, divided by the Liwu River, forming a breathtaking gorge. The site attracts visitors from all over the world who want to uncover the beauty of the mountains by hiking and exploring its many trails.

When the earthquake struck, it caused massive landslides within the National Park, resulting in casualties, injuries, damage to vehicles, and severe impact to infrastructure. Roads were blocked and cell reception was severed. As aftershocks continued, rescue efforts were affected.

Hundreds of people were trapped inside the National Park, with no means to connect with their families. They were left to survive from one day to the next on limited supplies of food and water, with no information about rescue timelines. My husband, Gautam, and I were 2 such people caught in the earthquake and trapped within a tunnel of Taroko National Park[2] for 24 hours before making a dangerous hike out.

This is our survival story. A journey through a brief period of life-threatening adversity. A story of perseverance, resilience, purpose and partnership. Of community, humanity, love and friendship. A story of gratitude, second chances and a reminder to celebrate each day.

– Namrata Kohli

Quotes from Readers

"...reading this account of a young woman caught with her soulmate in the eye of an earthquake, I shivered, shuddered, and smiled through tears."

~ Sangita Chaudhri, Gurgaon, India.

"Nam's perseverance in capturing the raw emotions of her experience is commendable. The honesty and depth of her writing evoke powerful feelings and made me choke up several times."

~ James Burnham, New York, United States.

"Nam's courage in being open, vulnerable, and raw in her memoir is truly inspiring. Her account beautifully illustrates the power of kindness and how small acts of courage can bring a glimmer of light and hope."

~ Diana A, Singapore.

"It is a remarkable piece of writing. A captivating and all-consuming narration of events and emotions. Knowing it is not a piece of fiction but a grim reality...for the emotional honesty shared here, I am compelled to describe it as a winsome read."

~ Seema Puri, Gurgaon, India.

"A very warm story that made me smile. It is a sincere, heartwarming tale of discovering new sides of life."

~ Alena Kondiurina, fellow survivor of the earthquake from Singapore.

"Namrata's account of our several-hour hike is riveting and true to life, as I relive it in my mind through her words."

~ Chris Fate, fellow survivor of the earthquake from Seattle, Washington, United States.

Foreword

This journey called life never fails to surprise. You set out for a long, languorous holiday, and then the very earth under your feet decides to play a prank or two—or more! From admiring pristine landscapes, you suddenly find yourself staring death in the face. The ensuing battle for life is the essence of this story.

Namrata's tale bears testimony to the universal human predicament: wishing for eternal existence while confronting the stark truth of human mortality. It is a story of faith conquering fear, with grit and endurance as allies. A story that teaches you gratitude and reaffirms your belief in the goodness of humankind.

From hearing my baby niece Namrata prattling off tales of Thumbelina and Goldilocks to reading this account of a young woman caught with her soulmate in the eye of an earthquake, I shivered, shuddered, and smiled through tears.

Namrata, I should have known—you are a born storyteller. You have just chronicled a story, a la 'Chicken Soup for the Adventurer's Soul.' Keep travelling, keep writing!

Sangita Chaudhri

Sangita Chaudhri is a retired English teacher from Sanskriti School, New Delhi. A theatre enthusiast and avid traveller, she enjoys scripting plays and writing travelogues. She lives in Gurugram, India.

As I reflected on my own experience during Taiwan's worst earthquake in 25 years, a pang of regret initially surfaced for not having truly connected with my fellow survivors. However, after delving into Namrata's gripping account in Shaken. Not Broken, I realised that our shared ordeal forged a connection between us that few others in this world will ever understand. In the span of 24 hours, it feels as though we lived a lifetime together.

Namrata's narrative, filled with raw emotion and unflinching honesty, provided me with a lens through which to process my own feelings and emotions. Through her eyes and heart, I found resonance with my own experience. This story of tragedy, survival, faith, and acceptance illuminates the depth of our shared humanity.

Now, I carry the vivid memories of Namrata, Gautam, and my fellow survivors with me, forging a connection that transcends the boundaries of time and distance. Were those days the worst or the best of our lives? The answer lies within the pages of this remarkable memoir. Keep reading to discover the truth that emerged from our collective journey.

Chris Fate

Chris Fate, a retired electric utility engineer residing in Seattle, Washington, was among the tourists caught in Taroko National Park. He joined Nam and her husband, Gautam, on a treacherous hike to safety after being trapped in a tunnel following the earthquake in Taiwan.

Preface

I am an ordinary person and I lead an ordinary life. I work a corporate job, meditate through the week, live for the weekends, experiment with baking, binge-watch TV shows, and look forward to a few relaxing holidays each year. One day, during what was supposed to be a fun-filled holiday, life hurled something extraordinary my way–not in a good sense. My husband and I came face to face with our mortality and fought for survival.

In the weeks following our return from surviving the earthquake in Taiwan, I was in a state of shock, grieving yet grateful. While it is far from the worst trauma anyone has ever experienced, it has undoubtedly been the most difficult time of my life. I began writing a journal to process what we went through. It started as a brain dump of everything I could remember and gradually evolved into a more detailed account.

Writing was the only way I could make sense of the emotional rollercoaster I was on–grateful one moment and heartbroken the next. As I wrote, I filled tens of pages with ease. Adding pictures brought me clarity and helped me understand my feelings. This process has been instrumental in my healing and recovery. What you will read here are essentially my journal entries–they are filled with my raw, unfiltered, and vulnerable emotions. This is me, turned inside out.

There is no reason to publish this book other than to show you that writing can be a powerful tool for healing. It has helped me overcome the trauma we experienced and see the silver linings in a very dark cloud. If you pick up this memoir, I hope it will keep you company on your journey through any hardship you may be experiencing. I hope it offers some inspiration to help you find your own way of processing your feelings.

I am deeply grateful that you have chosen to read this book. It is my attempt to transmute the fear and pain of surviving a harrowing ordeal into a creative offering. It is my pilgrimage of gratitude, hope, and love.

– **Nam,**
June 2024

Prologue

We held hands, and his first words were, "I think I've been hit." Only then did we realise that we stood on the edge of a cliff, next to a river flowing through towering mountains. We were in the wild, surrounded by nature's grandeur, witnessing landslides and rockfalls caused by shifting tectonic plates that could potentially change the course of the river or engulf the very ground we stood on.

"It's okay. We are okay. I love you. We are fine. It's going to be fine. I love you."

This was us in the minutes following the earthquake that struck as we were barely 10 kilometres from the epicentre in Taroko National Park's famous Tunnel of Nine Turns. What followed was a series of events we could never have imagined–the stuff of apocalyptic movies. During our seemingly idyllic holiday, my husband, Gautam, and I found ourselves thrust into a nightmare as we experienced Taiwan's most devastating earthquake in a quarter of a century.

We walked towards the starting point of the trail where our car was parked, to find everything enveloped in a dust haze. Still in a state of shock, we got into the car and attempted to drive out. But just a few metres in, we could barely see anything in the tunnel. The lights were out, and the dust was so dense that we had to stop and look at each other in disbelief.

What is going on? What in the world are we experiencing? Is this real, or is it a nightmare? Are we really going to be okay? What brought us to this situation in the first place? How on earth did we end up in Taiwan?

In the chapters ahead, I will detail what brought us to Taiwan and what we were doing in Taroko National Park on that fateful day. I will recount the moments following the earthquake and our struggle for survival, coping with the emotional turmoil that accompanied the physical dangers. I will share some of the lessons I gleaned from the experience–lessons in love, life, resilience, gratitude and a reminder to look for silver linings even in the darkest times.

PART 1

Of Dreams and Reality

Taiwan Unveiled

Taiwan had long held a coveted spot on my travel wish list, its allure of coastal cliffs, high-rise towers with rooftop bars, and a culinary scene that promised to tantalise the taste buds. For years, I had been enticing Gautam with the idea of a long weekend getaway, tempting him with visions of rugged hikes along coastal paths and immersive food and cultural experiences.

Yet, Gautam was not one for mere weekend getaways. If we were to embark on this journey, he insisted on delving deep into the heart of Taiwan, exploring its countryside, lakes, villages, and coastal towns. And so, 6 months before our intended travel dates, he meticulously crafted a plan—a 12-day exploration of Taiwan, spanning 2 long-weekends, promising a journey of discovery.

Our adventure began on a Friday, with Taipei as our inaugural destination. The city pulsated with energy, its metro stations bustling with activity and its streets throbbing with life. We immersed ourselves in the vibrant culture, navigating long queues at popular eateries and sampling delicacies at popular green onion pancakes and coffee stalls.

We explored the grandeur of the Chiang Kai-Shek Memorial Hall, with its imposing white marble structure and vibrant blue tiled roof set against the backdrop of meticulously landscaped gardens. The expansive Liberty Square surrounding the memorial provided a peaceful space to absorb the historical significance of the site and Chiang Kai-shek's legacy.

Taipei Chiang Kai-Shek Memorial Hall

Beautiful Temples of Taipei

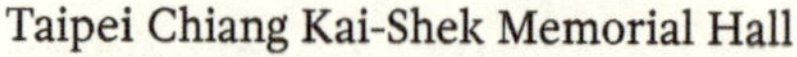

The night markets of Taipei cast a spell, their alleys alive with the aroma of stinky tofu mingling with the sweetness of tanghulu and nougat. As I marvelled at the game arcades, a wave of nostalgia swept over me, carrying me back to the carefree days of my childhood. I couldn't help but wonder how incredible it would have been if my brother and I had such attractions within reach when we were children. It would have been the time of our lives, filled with laughter, competition, and endless fun.

We savoured each bite, relishing in the genius of mung bean smoothies and native pork buns. Venturing off the beaten path, we sought out hidden soymilk shops and queued patiently at local hawkers, where we had to rely on translation apps to read the menu to place an order. The challenge was what made it worthwhile—we were determined to experience Taiwan not as tourists, but as locals.

Fuzhou Pepper Buns (Hujiao Bing) at Raohe Night Market. Pork buns made in a tandoor oven. Ridiculously delicious!

Fresh squid and octopus ready for the grill. Served with a delightful array of sauces

Rainbow crosswalk in Ximen district

Queues at Shilin night market

In the Ximen district, we were enamoured by the Taiwanese youth's fascination with anime, as they queued for hours to participate in a lucky draw. Meanwhile, we lost ourselves in the labyrinth of arcades with claw crane kiosks to try our luck to pull out an iPhone—a few unsuccessful attempts that brought much laughter and joy.

We paid a visit to Longshan Temple, one of Taipei's most revered cultural landmarks. The temple's ornate architecture and intricate carvings were mesmerising, with each detail telling a story of tradition. We observed locals and visitors alike lighting incense and offering prayers, contributing to the serene ambience. I wandered through the temple grounds and felt a deep connection to Taipei's rich cultural and spiritual heritage.

Yet, as captivating as Taipei was, the countryside beckoned. After 3 exhilarating days in the city, we eagerly set out on the next leg of our journey—a road trip that promised to reveal Taiwan's natural splendour. Our destination: Xincheng, a quaint town nestled by Hualien, serving as our gateway to Taroko National Park.

With the hum of the city fading behind us, we embraced the open road, eager to breathe in the crisp mountain air and immerse ourselves in the serenity of Taiwan's untamed landscapes. The adventure had only just begun, and already, we were captivated by the promise of what lay ahead.

Taroko National Park

8 AM - 5 PM on Tuesday, 2-Apr 2024.

Taroko National Park is Taiwan's east coast's top tourist attraction. Covering 1200 square kilometres, rising from sea level to over 3,700 metres, it incorporates 27 peaks over 3,000 metres. Almost all of Taiwan's bio-geographical zones are represented here, along with half the island's plant species. But most visitors, including us, come to see one area—the 18-kilometre-long Taroko Gorge, whose marble walls rise out of the blue-green Liwu River, with a crowded backdrop of green mountainsides soaring above and several enticing hiking trails clinging to the cliff edges. It is one of Asia's scenic wonders, and we were there to experience that wonder first-hand.

Aerial View of a section of the Taroko Gorge

History of Taroko: Literally meaning magnificent or beautiful in Truku—an indigenous language spoken in the mountains of Northern Taiwan—the Taroko area began as coral deposits, compressed beneath an ancient sea which was transformed by aeons of geology into limestone and then marble, schists and gneiss. Some 5 million years ago, Taiwan started lifting from the sea as the Philippine and Eurasian plates collided. Water erosion then carved out softer deposits to leave the towering canyon walls of harder rock.

Our exploration of Taroko began on a crisp morning, fuelled by anticipation and a picnic bag packed with eggs and cheese sandwiches. Day 1 of our adventure unfolded with a series of unforgettable experiences along the park's most renowned trails:

Qingshui cliff, enroute to Hualien

Entrance to Shakadang Trail

Shakadang Trail

An easy journey through a deep-cut side valley, tracing the crystal-clear waters of the Shakadang River as egrets fished in turquoise pools while cicadas and frogs competed to out-sing stretches of gurgling rapids.

Taroko Gorge

The crown jewel of the National Park, this 18 km marble-walled gorge, captivated us with its splendour, inviting us to hike its trails, and marvel at its geological wonders, as we drove along the road that traversed its length, agape at the towering mountains that seemed to float vertiginously above us.

Swallow Grotto

Beckoning with its winding roads and rock-cut pillars, the Swallow Grotto trail provided a glimpse into the park's geological past and offered breathtaking views of the canyon below.

Taroko Gorge on a clear day

Bulowan Suspension Bridge

Bulowan Suspension Bridge

A feat of engineering, this bridge connected 2 mountains across the gorge at dizzying heights, offering dazzling views of the surrounding landscape.

Baiyang Trail

Our day culminated with a 4 km trail through multiple unlit pedestrian tunnels, leading to a viewpoint overlooking sections of the Baiyang

Waterfall, which cascades from faults in a tunnel, creating a magical scene.

Unlit pedestrian tunnel that starts the eerie Baiyang trail

With 2 pending trails awaiting our exploration on the following day, our journey through Taroko was not yet complete. From the Tunnel of Nine Turns to the Lushui Trail, each one promised to reveal a different facet of this natural wonderland, leaving us in awe of the majesty that surrounded us.

Tunnel of Nine Turns (*Jiuqudong*)

Considered one of the most scenic sections of Taroko Gorge, the trail itself is 700m in length, and the tunnel meanders high along the mountains, where you can experience an impressive view of the Liwu River from an imposing height.

Lushui Trail

The perfect starting point to see waterfalls, a green forest and several suspension bridges along the way with grand sweeping views down the peak-studded gorge.

Happiest Day of Our Lives

6 PM on Tuesday, 2-Apr 2024.

Our first day of adventure in Taroko was a day filled with exploration and discovery among the trails of the National Park. Exhausted from our trek, we decided to take it easy and enjoy a quiet evening in the quaint village near our Airbnb. Just a short stroll away, a picturesque promenade hugged the coastline, where the Pacific Ocean met the mouth of the Liwu River.

It was against this tranquil backdrop that Gautam posed a question that would linger in our minds long after the sun had set. "What is the happiest day of your life?" he asked, prompting me to delve deep into the recesses of my memory.

In my contemplation of his query, a whirlwind of moments flooded my thoughts–instances of memories shared with loved ones, triumphs at work, and personal achievements. Each memory carried its own weight of joy, yet none seemed to stand out as the epitome of happiness. The complexities of the mind became apparent as I realised how fleeting happiness can be, how easily overshadowed by worries of the future or regrets of the past.

Turning the question back to Gautam, I found that he too struggled to pinpoint a single day as the happiest of his life. And so, we shifted our focus to a different inquiry: "What is the worst day of your life?"

The answer, if there even was one, remained elusive as we contemplated the highs and lows that shape our existence. Perhaps the true significance lay not in the specific days themselves but in the journey they represent–a mosaic of experiences, emotions, and lessons learned.

So, I pose the question to you: Do you have an answer?

As you reflect on the peaks and valleys of your own life, consider the significance of each moment and the stories they tell. And perhaps, like us, you will find that the beauty lies not in the destination but in the winding path that leads us there.

Jiuqudong: The Tunnel with Nine Turns

7:30 AM on Wednesday, 3-Apr 2024.

The second day of our Taroko adventure greeted us with a picturesque scene painted by vibrant blue skies and radiant sunshine. With rejuvenating rest following a day of hiking, our spirits were high, though our legs still bore the pleasant fatigue of yesterday's endeavours. As we contemplated the day ahead, we faced a choice: to take a leisurely approach or to embark on one final exploration of Taroko's wonders.

Swayed by a desire to savour the tranquility of the park while ensuring we did not miss its most renowned trail–the Tunnel of Nine Turns–we opted for a compromise. With a breakfast picnic basket along with a steaming flask of coffee and refreshing lemonade, we set out early to beat the crowds and seize the day's adventures.

As our car made its way through Taroko's winding roads, a sense of contentment washed over me. The majestic beauty of the park, with its towering cliffs and lush greenery, evoked a feeling of awe and appreciation. Capturing the moment for Instagram[3], we journeyed onward, oblivious to the wonders or dangers awaiting us.

7:35 AM Upon reaching the Tunnel of Nine Turns, we made an audacious decision to park within the restricted zone, ignoring the 'No Parking' signs to allow a smooth exploration of the trail. With a plan to complete the 700-metre hike in record time, we set off eagerly, ready to immerse ourselves in Taroko's most popular natural wonder.

As we ventured into the semi-covered tunnel, we walked through remnants of the old highway that was repurposed into a scenic trail. We marvelled at the geological formations and cascading waterfalls that adorned our path. The rugged beauty of the gorge, with its towering cliffs and glistening river below, left us spellbound at every turn.

Jiuqudong trail lets you get a close view of geological formations of Taroko Gorge

Rugged beauty of the gorge, with its towering cliffs and glistening river below

7:46 AM Bathed in the golden glow of the sun, we delighted in the solitude of our surroundings, savouring the chance to experience Taroko's splendour in peace. With only a *lone jogger* crossing our path, we felt privileged to have this slice of paradise all to ourselves.

7:48 AM Though our journey was cut short by a closed section of the trail, our hearts brimmed with contentment and gratitude for the moments we had shared with nature. As we bid farewell to the mountains, I paused to touch the cool marble rock, seeking blessings in the age-old tradition of the natives. With a final selfie capturing the breathtaking vista behind us, we departed, ready to find the perfect spot for our well-deserved picnic.

Thrilled to have the entire trail with these majestic views all to ourselves

Seeking blessings from the mountain Gods before we started to make our way back

PART 2

Shaken to the Core

When the Earth Shook

7:58 AM on Wednesday, 3-Apr 2024.

Unaware of Taiwan's origins in the restless churn of tectonic plates, I strolled towards the car, typing a response to a friend's text.

Suddenly, a rumble rose from the earth, a deep growl akin to standing atop a furious, enraged beast. Just as the ground began to tremble beneath me, Gautam, a few paces behind, exclaimed, "Oh shit, EARTHQUAKE!" as his phone buzzed with a presidential alert.

Presidential alert warning on our phones

As the tremors intensified, we RAN. I cannot recall how long we ran or in which direction. My legs trembled as though they had developed a superpower. I was being propelled by instinct towards safety as the ground convulsed beneath us. Eventually, I could no longer see, so I stopped to ensure Gautam remained close.

We held hands, and his first words were, "I think I've been hit." Only then did we realise that we stood on the edge of a cliff, flanked by towering mountains, 3,000 metres high with a coursing river flowing through. In the heart of nature's vast unpredictability, we were witnessing landslides and rockfalls caused by tectonic turmoil that had the potential to change the course of the river or engulf the very mountain we stood on.

Rocks had started cascading like bullets, and one struck Gautam like a meteor, slicing his ear lobe and jaw. In the dust-choked valley, darkness descended in the morning light, painting a scene of impending doom. Dark clouds of dust flooded every square centimetre of space as we held onto each other tight, so tight.

Fear had an equally tight grip on us—an overwhelming dread of death, pain, and separation from each other and loved ones. We clung to each other, tightly bound, memories of happier times flashing through my mind. I whispered a prayer of gratitude to the universe, professing love for my family and seeking their blessings.

All I could think of was, 'It's okay, we're okay. This will pass,' but another voice said, 'This is it. This is how it is going to end.' Feeling a complete loss of control, I was terrified at that moment. I continued to pray for the tremors to pass. All along, telling Gautam, "It's okay. We're okay, I love you. It's fine. It's going to be fine."

We did not know this at the time, but fortune smiled upon us as we found shelter in a small alcove amidst the chaos. We had stopped in a cave-like structure, open on both sides. Here, the rocks falling on either side bounced off the floor onto our ankles, calves and knees, but the overhang shielded our heads, sparing us from significant harm.

Minutes stretched into eternity before the deluge subsided. Blinking through dust-choked air, I illuminated our surroundings with my phone's torch. Edging cautiously, staying close to the mountain, we walked hand in hand in the direction of the car, hoping to drive out of there.

Just our luck, we were about 200 metres away from the start of the trail. Being the most popular and accessible trail in Taroko, this tunnel was equipped with toilets and a small guardhouse at the entrance. Despite our terror, we went into the toilets to wash the dust and blood from Gautam's wound. I pressed the emergency button in a desperate bid for help, but no one responded.

Mindful not to linger due to the continued risk of rockfall, we walked back towards the car in utter disbelief at what we had just experienced.

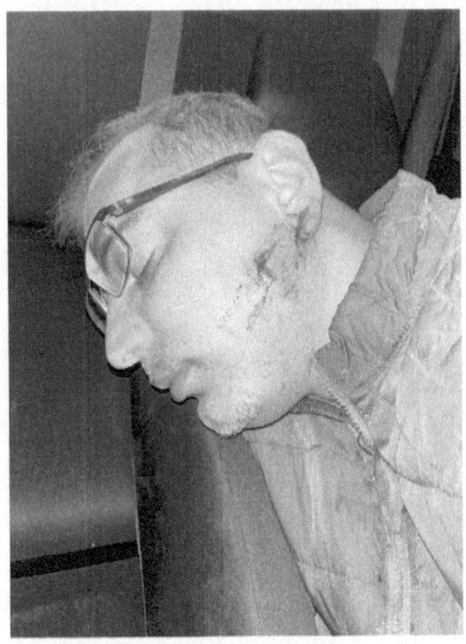

Gautam injured, left face hit by a rock that came like a meteor

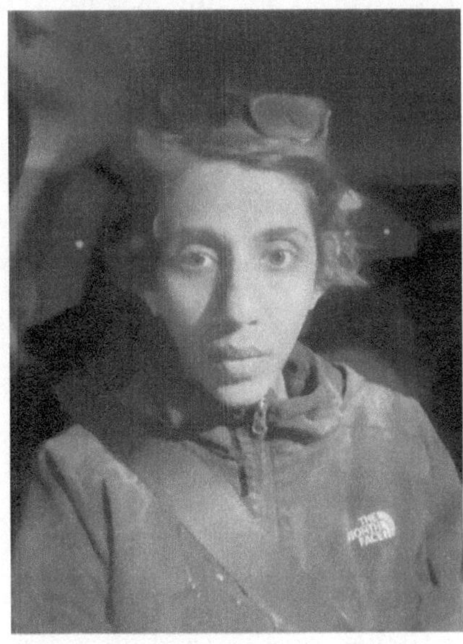

First selfie taken after the earthquake

The Other People in Jiuqudong

8:05 AM

As we stepped into the starting point of the trail in the Tunnel of Nine Turns, it was enveloped in a dust haze. Across the road, 2 figures emerged from the haze.

"Are you okay?" I called out, though language formed a barrier between us.

They seemed unharmed and asked if we were okay. I indicated that Gautam was hurt, but we were determined to keep moving and hoped to drive out of the park.

Still reeling from shock, we made our way to the car. Covered in a thick layer of dust, visibility through the windshield was nearly non-existent. Nevertheless, we fumbled for the ignition and set off, but where to? Barely 100 metres into the tunnel, darkness swallowed us whole. Dust hung heavy in the air, obscuring our surroundings. With no destination in sight, we came to an abrupt stop, exchanging bewildered glances in silent disbelief.

What in the world were we witnessing? We took a moment to check in with each other.

"Are you okay?"

"I'm okay. It's okay."

"I love you. We are going to be okay."

But beneath the surface, unease lingered. With trembling hands, we flicked on the car lights, illuminating our dust-covered faces in the dim glow. Physically, Gautam bore the brunt of the ordeal, his injuries evident as blood gushed from his left face and earlobe. As for myself, I was merely covered in dust, but the emotional toll ran deep.

I craned my neck to survey the surroundings. I noticed several more figures emerging cautiously from behind pillars and the wreckage of a shattered minivan. Physically unharmed yet unmistakably shaken, we shared a collective sense of bewilderment. What had just unfolded before our eyes?

Among the people were local residents of Taiwan, their calm demeanour belying the chaos of the situation. Raised in an environment where seismic activity was a part of life, they possessed a deep-rooted familiarity with earthquakes. From a young age, they had been educated on the necessary precautions and trained to respond swiftly to such events.

However, despite their composure, there was an underlying desperation in their actions.

They instinctively gravitated towards safety by seeking refuge in the confines of the tunnel, acknowledging it as the most secure haven in such a crisis. Yet, even for those accustomed to the tremors of the earth, the magnitude of the recent quake was unprecedented. One among them had travelled this very road daily for 2 decades, yet had never encountered such devastation. While they were adept at seeking cover during tremors, none had witnessed this level of destruction, such a close shave in their life.

Everyone was desperate to find a way out—to get in contact with their family and tell them they were safe. But there was no cell signal, no network reception. No electricity. We were officially cut off from the outside world; the tunnel had become our enclave, each other our only solace.

In our shared shock, a sense of unity emerged. A woman approached our car, offering basic first aid for Gautam's injury. She had alcohol wipes, antiseptic ointment and double-action pain relief medication. She offered us water and some rationing advice–a lifeline in our newfound isolation. She suggested that we turn off the car engine and lights.

With resources scarce, we heeded their counsel to conserve.

The tunnel, they affirmed, was our safest refuge; any attempts to leave would be futile.

"How long?" I inquired, met with uncertainty.

"I don't know," she admitted. "At least a day, maybe 2, maybe more..."

Navigating Grief in a Time of Crisis

9:00 AM

We had traversed the initial stage of grief–the **shock**, the disbelief, the utter confusion engulfing us in the aftermath of our ordeal. Without even a moment to process, we were thrust into the next phase: **denial.**

"We will get out of here," I insist to myself, to Gautam, to the universe at large. "We have a car. We will drive until we find safety. We will go as far as the car takes us and then walk out of the National Park."

Then, the first aftershock rattles our fragile hope. We did not know at the time that it was a 5.2 magnitude earthquake. But we know what we felt–it was the same rumbling, as the car shuddered in the tunnel and echoes of falling debris reverberated through the metal confines, reminding us of the doom.

Thud. Clang. Crunch. Whack. Crack. Whang.

Anger simmers beneath the surface. 'Why us? Why today, when we are on a holiday? What did we do to deserve this?' I rail against the injustice of our circumstances. "We should never have come out," I mutter, only to be interrupted by yet another aftershock. The same build-up of rumbling and the cycle repeats, each tremor eroding our resolve, leaving behind only raw fear. It quickly became apparent that we were not going to have the luxury of time to process anything at that moment.

And so, we enter the **bargaining** phase. "When will this end?" I plead with fate, karma and destiny. I plead with any higher power that may be listening. "I'll change. I'll be better, I'll give up bad habits, talk to my family regularly and tell them I love them," I promise, desperate for reprieve.

But each aftershock shatters our illusions of control, leaving us to confront the harsh reality of our situation. Each time, the earth goes *grrrrrr*, like a train fast approaching or a plane about to take off. Then the ground beneath us trembles, and I am convinced that this time, it will not hold. It is going to cave; the weight of the mountain is going to fall and engulf us to be buried alive.

Thud. Clang. Crunch. Whack. Crack. Whang.

Depression washes over me like a suffocating wave. "Is this how it ends?" I wonder aloud, resigned to our fate. Yet, through the despair, a glimmer of acceptance begins to emerge. It's alright. Maybe we ought to be thankful to have this extra time to tell each other 'I love you.' Perhaps it is too much to expect any more from this life.

Eventually, we reach **acceptance**. If we are going to be here for the next 3 days, we will need to budget supplies–food, water, medication and power. We take stock of what little we have: cheese sandwiches, eggs packed for our picnic, 2 sticks of nougat purchased from the night market, a snicker bar, a flask of lemonade, a thermos of black coffee and half a bag of leftover dark chocolate orange granola, courtesy of my weekend baking experiments, lying in the car.

We had 2 bottles of water, a car with half a tank of fuel and a USB charging cable–in case we ran out of battery. But most importantly, we had the car–a haven providing a sheltered place to sit, to rest and to keep warm through the night. With no communication with the outside world, no knowledge of when–or if–rescue will come, we had to prepare ourselves for the long haul.

Each aftershock served as a harsh reminder of our vulnerability, of nature's unrelenting power. If we were going to make it out of there alive, we were going to need the physical stamina and mental resilience to endure...

Regret, Gratitude and Anxiety Coexist

10:29 AM

For the next few hours, Gautam and I remained confined to the car, makeshift bandages made from toilet paper and my sweatband tending to his wound as he reclined the car seat to stem the bleeding. In the eerie silence, our minds become cacophonous with thoughts–regret, gratitude, anxiety–each vying for attention in the dim confines of our sanctuary.

A bazillion thoughts flood my mind: Family. Work. Life and at that moment, I think of a meeting I know I won't be able to make and cannot inform of my absentia. Then a balancing thought: it's okay, we are alright. It could have been much worse. It's like we have a second life.

Regret. How on earth did we end up at this harrowing juncture?

This was not part of the plan. We were on vacation. Surely, such things cannot happen to those on a holiday. Holidays are when we take a break from life! Life is when things go wrong. Holidays are exempt from bad things. Everyone knows that!

We were supposed to do a leisurely hike, have a picnic and then spend a relaxing day by the lake. We should never have come out here. But how could we ever have known?

Regret. When did I last speak to my parents? How did we end that call? Did I tell them I love them?

Regret. We nearly died today. What would be my biggest regret if we died?

First reactions yield to acceptance, a quiet acknowledgement of the fragility of our existence. If this were our curtain call, what better way to bid adieu than together, immersed in nature?

Yet, concern for our family's anguish tugs at our hearts, compounded by our severed communication with the outside world. If only I could send them a text to let them know we were okay. I tried to send a message, but there was no cell service.

Anxiety tightens its grip. Are we really going to be okay? How badly is Gautam hurt? Will we make it out of here alive? Another aftershock. Rocks continue to fall. The car shakes violently in the tunnel. We look at each other, hold hands and take this chance to tell each other again.

"I love you. It's okay. If this is how it's going to end, there is no one else I would rather be with and no place else I would choose. I love you."

How are we ever going to make it out of here? We are physically safe, but trapped at the mouth of a 4 km-long tunnel. We know it is not over, far from it.

In front of us, we can see the extent of destruction brought by the landslides. What was once a smooth, clean road is now piled with feet of fallen rocks and debris from the mountain. Every few minutes as the wind picks up or another tremor hits, more rocks fall, trees collapse, more metal, dust, and stones pile on. The avalanche of rockfall has now become a steady rainfall. There is no way we can get out of here on our own.

We could try the other side of the tunnel, but it is too dark. There is no electricity, and the dust sits heavy, making it very difficult to see even with fog lights. We cannot walk, and it is difficult to breathe with all that dust. The park exit is another 15 kilometres away, and the terrain is treacherous.

Yet, in the uncertainty and trepidation flickered a glimmer of resilience–a determination to endure, to persevere, bound by love and a shared resolve to weather the storm together. And so, we braced ourselves, steeling our spirits for the trials that lay ahead, clinging to hope in the encroaching darkness. We checked our food inventory and realised we hadn't had anything to eat since dinner the previous day. Thank goodness we packed for a picnic and managed to reach our car...

Thankful for the What-ifs and Not-ifs

11:00 AM

As the reality of our situation began to sink in, we found ourselves gradually accepting the dire circumstances we were in. After the initial whirlwind of regret and anxiety, a tidal wave of guilt washed over me.

I could not help but feel remorse for the countless times I had turned a blind eye to disasters unfolding in far-flung corners of the world, dismissing them as mere blips on the radar of our lives. It was a sobering realisation that despite my empathy, I had often failed to truly comprehend the magnitude of such tragedies. How many times had we shrugged off the suffering of others, cocooned in the comfort of our own existence?

In spite of the guilt, this was a reminder of life's fragility. We only have one shot at this journey, one chance to embrace each moment with purpose and meaning. It was a reminder that even in the face of uncertainty, every breath is a gift to be cherished.

My thoughts drifted to the countless individuals caught in the throes of terror and natural calamities, their faces and names lost in the annals of tragedy. What must they endure? How do they find the strength to carry on? Would we ever be able to shake off the weight of this ordeal, should we be fortunate enough to emerge unharmed?

In the midst of uncertainty, my mind sought refuge in modelling alternate scenarios, each one more harrowing than the last. What if the earthquake had struck at a different moment? What if we had been in a more dangerous position, without the safety of our car or the company of fellow travellers?

- The earthquake could have struck yesterday, when we were on the Shakadang Trail. A 4 km stretch against a vertical mountain cliff with no tunnels or other places of refuge. I thought back to any hikers who might be at Shakadang Trail and said a prayer for them.
- The earthquake could have struck the following hour when we were either driving or having a picnic at our chosen scenic spot. And if we did not know how to recognise the alarm sounds, it would have been our car that was engulfed by a massive boulder from a landslide.[4]
- We could be 2 kilometres deep into the Baiyang trail, as we were just yesterday afternoon, with no car, no food or water to sustain an entire day or more.
- We could have been at a picnic spot around Swallow Grotto with no other people in sight. I don't know how we would have reacted, or the decisions we would have made with no other people around.
- Or we could have been 5 metres in either direction on the very same trail we were on and been hit by a bigger rock, getting seriously injured or hurt. If we did not stop for exactly that much time to take pictures and appreciate the views, our reality today would be very different.
- On the other hand, if we listened to our tired muscles and decided to take it easy, we might still be lazing at our Airbnb and been spared the entire ordeal.

But dwelling on the what-ifs served no purpose. We could not change the past or control the future. All we have is the present moment, and it is in this moment that we must find gratitude, even in adversity.

With this newfound perspective, we made a conscious effort to express appreciation for the blessings we still possessed. Despite the mayhem surrounding us, we were okay. We had basic sustenance—food and water to nourish our bodies. Our car provided a haven of warmth and shelter. And most importantly, we were not alone. We had each other—companions to share the journey and to lean on in times of need.

Even the small comforts took on new significance. Access to toilets may seem trivial in ordinary circumstances, but in our current reality, it afforded us a semblance of dignity in the chaos. We counted our blessings.

We couldn't help but acknowledge how much worse things could have been. We were grateful for the chance to still hold each other close to whisper words of love and reassurance. We clung to each other, grateful for the chance to share another day, another breath. In the end, it is the moments of connection and love that truly matter, both in times of peace and while confronting adversity.

Finding My Reason to Survive

Let me tell you a little about myself–I am a storyteller at heart. I have a deep fascination with tales of resilience, of humanity rising above adversity and finding purpose in hardship. Whether it is through books, movies, or documentaries, I am drawn to stories that showcase the indomitable spirit of the human soul.

One book that holds a special place in my heart is 'Man's Search for Meaning' by Viktor Frankl. It chronicles his harrowing experiences in Nazi concentration camps during World War II and explores the concept of finding meaning in life, even in unimaginable suffering. Frankl's insights into human resilience left a lasting impression on me.

Now, onto a slightly different note–my husband and I often engage in rather morbid discussions about life and death. One topic that frequently arises is how long we would want to live if we ever reached a point of physical dependence on others. While my husband prefers to maintain his independence, I have always believed that life's most compelling stories unfold in moments of vulnerability and imperfection.

If you follow me on Instagram, you have probably noticed that I love to share snippets of my life, no matter how mundane they may seem. 5-kilometre hike? New recipe experiment? New workout? It is all there. There is a part of me that craves connection, that delights in finding an audience for my musings. But despite my love for storytelling, I haven't written as much as I would like to.

Here is why: I have always considered my own life and upbringing to be relatively unremarkable. I hail from a loving family that provided stability and support throughout my childhood. I was a devoted student. Pre-reads and homework were diligently completed, and I was always eager to excel in the classroom and impress the teachers.

Though we weren't wealthy, we made the most of what we had, creating memories on family vacations and bonding over shared adventures. We would pack our family of 5, including our pet boxer dog named Doller (not a typo), into a hatchback car. I watched my cousins climb trees, pluck raw mangoes for a freshly made aam panna (a refreshing sweet and salty drink like lemonade) in the summer, or make friends with reptile pets–a frog or a lizard in the monsoons.

However, it wasn't until I found myself caught in the commotion of Taiwan's worst earthquake in decades that I realised the potential for my own story to unfold. Trapped in a National Park during the quake, spending nights huddled in a tunnel, and embarking on a gnarly hike to safety–these experiences were unlike anything I had ever imagined I would go through.

Between the uncertainty and fear, I clung to the hope that I would survive to tell this story. This was my moment to find my voice, to bear witness to my own resilience and that of the human spirit in the face of adversity. With that resolve burning within me, I held onto the belief that I would emerge from this ordeal with a story worth telling–I was going to get out of there alive.

PART 3

The Tunnel of Trials

The Forgotten Hiker

11:08 AM

Ah, chapter 4–how could I forget? In the chaos of our own predicament, there was one detail that slipped our minds entirely. Remember the lone hiker we encountered on the Jiuqudong trail during our morning walk? It wasn't until one of us recalled his presence that a sinking feeling settled in.

In an instant, our expressions mirrored the same thought: 'Uh Oh.' We hadn't spared a second thought for him, lost in our own nightmare. We had seen him over 3 hours ago, heading deeper into the trail. The thought of his safety weighed on our minds.

Determined to alert the others, I stepped out of the car to convey this information to the group. As I spoke, their expressions darkened noticeably.

"Was he a local Taiwanese or a foreigner?" they inquired, their concern palpable.

"I can't say for certain, but he seemed more like a foreigner," I replied. His jungle hat and khaki attire, coupled with his early morning jog on a touristy trail, suggested as much.

Upon hearing this, the faces of the locals grew sombre. The destruction wrought by the earthquake was evident, and the reality dawned on us–all those caught in its path, including the lone hiker, faced an unthinkable situation.

Broken mountain face and debris piled up on a damaged section of the trail where the lone hiker was stranded

We strained our eyes, calling out into the distance, hoping for a response. "Hello! Can you hear me? Is anybody there?" But the echoes of our voices faded into the silence of the wilderness. Given the ongoing aftershocks and landslides, attempting a rescue mission was extremely risky, if not impossible.

Then, after what felt like an eternity, a figure emerged at the end of the trail. Gasps of relief rippled through the group as we noticed that someone was walking out.

"He is alive! Someone is walking out!" I dashed out to see if it was the hiker.

Bloody and bruised, the same man we saw on the trail was walking into the tunnel with his clothes stained by blood and dust. His hands and legs were peppered with wounds where he was pelted by falling rocks. Wounds on his face were clotted by dust, and his eyes were bloodshot. He was immediately surrounded by people who were checking in to make sure he was okay. But they did not speak each other's language. As someone who had spent the past few hours communicating in part English and part charades with this crew, I stepped in to translate.

The man was in a state of shock, but physically he was okay. He was hurt, but he walked out by himself. He sat outside the guard room while onlookers frantically whipped out their cell phones to take pictures of his condition. He explained that he was quite far into the trail when the earthquake struck. As the rocks started to fall, he stepped as close to the mountain as he could, facing the mountain, and used his arms to cover his face and head as the rocks continued to fall, bouncing off the floor around him and hitting his legs and back.

After the first major quake stopped, he stayed there for an hour, calculating his chances of survival versus the possibility of rescue teams reaching him. Going by the extent of the damage and the frequency of aftershocks, it became clear that help was at least a few days away. Powered by an instinct for survival and driven by adrenaline, he took some calculated risks and made the decision to walk out of the trail and into the tunnel. It was not an easy road back, but he rolled the dice, and it paid off.

The guard brought out a first-aid kit and offered to clean up and bandage his wounds. To my surprise, he refused help, explaining that the wound had dried and blood was clotted with dust. Cleaning to administer first aid would result in bleeding again. He intended to walk out of the National Park and then seek medical attention, so he'd rather keep it as is. Just like that, paying no heed to advice, he decided to start walking further into the tunnel with the intention of exiting.

The security guard had a scooter parked in the tunnel. Uri, one of our fellow captives in the tunnel, offered to ferry this man to the other end of the tunnel on the scooter, to save him the 4 km walk out. When he returned, having dropped the man at the other end of the tunnel, Uri had discovered that the tunnel had a generator room with a half tank of gasoline that could possibly last a few hours of electricity. If only we could figure out how to turn it on...

Seeking Solutions in the Tunnel

12:37 PM

By now, it had been a few hours since the earthquake rattled our world, leaving us stranded in the tunnel with nowhere to go. We had resigned ourselves to the reality that the tunnel would be our home for the foreseeable future. When the earth shook, and the rocks tumbled, the landslides wreaked havoc on the cell towers and internet cables in and around Taroko/Hualien. This meant that for as long as we were confined to the tunnel, we would have no contact with the outside world. No way to reassure our families that we were safe and no way to seek information about the extent of the earthquake's impact.

All we had was each other–a group of individuals from all walks of life, speaking different languages and possessing various skills. Some were wait staff from the Silks Place Hotel in Taroko, and one was a driver who was ferrying the crew to the hotel via a mini-bus when the earthquake caused landslides on their path. They were lucky to be right outside the tunnel when the earthquake struck, and the driver had the presence of mind to retreat into the tunnel.[5]

Another member of the mini-bus crew was an IT guy, and we even had a cook among us.

Two people spoke a few words of English, while our Mandarin vocabulary was limited to just one word. Yet, I was certain that each person had something unique to offer. We all possessed valuable skills that could contribute to our survival. Though unsure of my own role in this community, I was determined to find my place and make a meaningful contribution.

I stepped out of the car and began engaging with the group, employing a combination of English and charades to glean as much information as possible. My initial attempts to use a translation app failed due to the absence of connectivity.

'How have we come to be so dependent on technology?' I wondered.

Nevertheless, I bombarded them with questions, desperate for any insight into our situation.

"Are earthquakes common in Taiwan?" I inquired, to which I received a solemn nod in response.

"Yes, the island of Taiwan was formed as a result of earthquakes. They are a common occurrence here," came the reply.

I was astonished by my own ignorance. How had I not known this? It was a wake-up call to be more informed and proactive when embarking on trips. Usually, I left all the planning to Gautam, but perhaps it was time to take a more active role in our adventures.

As the conversation unfolded, I learned that no one could tell the magnitude of the earthquake, making comparisons difficult. Some had lived in Taiwan for 2 decades without experiencing anything like this before. Speculations about the duration of our confinement swirled, with estimates ranging from days to weeks.

"How can we get more information about this earthquake—its magnitude, epicentre etc.?" I enquired.

"Cell towers were impacted, and phone lines were cut during the earthquake. It is going to be at least a few days before connectivity is restored. So, our best bet is to await rescue." they said.

Desperate for any semblance of connection, we scoured the tunnel for signs of hope. It was then that Uri, the IT guy among us, made a discovery—a few boxes tucked away in a corner of the tunnel. Among them were a telephone box, a DB fuse box, and a generator room about halfway into the tunnel.

One after another, each box was opened. Buttons pushed, signs scrutinised, followed by a sequence of additional button presses. Silence. A phone receiver was lifted. "Hello?" Silence.

Luck did not appear to be on our side so readily. Nonetheless, in moments like these, minds crave to be occupied, and able bodies demand activity.

Eager to utilise this newfound resource, a makeshift taskforce comprised of "IT experts" was assembled. The group included Gautam, who has had a knack for troubleshooting tech since his teenage days. I accompanied them on a trip to the generator room. The mission: to activate the generator and provide light and power for the night ahead. Armed with nothing but our cell phone torch and a rudimentary understanding of Chinese characters to read instructions, we embarked on a series of trial-and-error attempts to activate the machinery.

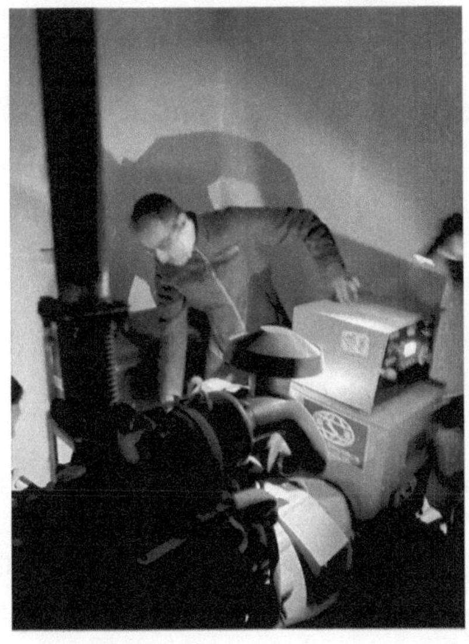

Inside the Generator Room

IT taskforce in action, translating instructions from Chinese-to-English

Real-time Chinese-to-English translations led to the first attempt to turn on the generator.

Click. Whir. Click. Ching Ching Ching. Brrrrr.

Fuse. Off.

Nothing.

Let's try this one more time.

Click. Whir. Click. Ching Ching Ching. Brrrrr.

Fuse. Off.

Same. Maybe we can try a choke? There is a button which we pull out. Give it a few seconds and then go again.

Same.

Perhaps another combination of buttons?

Each click and whir filled the air with anticipation, only to be met with disappointment as the generator remained stubbornly silent.

Maybe we need to make some changes to the output boxes.

Nothing.

One more attempt.

Click. Whir. Click. Ching Ching Ching. Brrrrr.

Brrrrrr. Shrill sound.

Alarm beeps. *Beeep beeep beeep beeep.*

The alarm continued to blare, its intensity escalating with each piercing beep. A wave of panic swept through our makeshift taskforce. With each shrill sound, my heart hammered against my chest, and a sense of dread settled over me. 'Not again,' I thought.

In the dimly lit generator room, surrounded by unfamiliar machinery and cryptic instructions, fear gnawed at the edges of my mind.

'What had we done wrong? Had our tinkering inadvertently triggered a catastrophic chain reaction? Was the generator on the brink of exploding, engulfing us and the mountain in its destruction?'

Frantic thoughts raced through my mind as I grappled with the overwhelming urge to flee. Every instinct screamed at me to abandon our efforts and seek safety outside the tunnel. But as the alarm blared relentlessly, drowning out all rational thought, I found myself paralysed by indecision.

Should we run? Should we stay and find a way to fix this? The weight of uncertainty bore down upon us, casting a pall of dread over our desperate situation. In that moment of chaos and confusion, all we could do was brace ourselves for whatever came next.

Three more beeps, and then it stopped. Phew!

Eventually, faced with the possibility of a catastrophe, we abandoned our efforts, resigning ourselves to a night without power.

Despite the uncertainty and disappointment, there was hope—a half tank of fuel in the car, with headlights to illuminate our path in the darkness. As the sun dipped below the horizon, we would huddle together, grateful for the flickering light of our cell phone torches and the warmth of human connection.

First Encounter with People from Outside the Tunnel

1:00 PM

On the way back from the generator room, the car's headlights cast a feeble beam through the thick veil of dust suspended in the air. Dust particles stood still in the beams, obscuring our vision and creating an eerie atmosphere within the tunnel. Despite the fog lights piercing through the darkness, visibility remained severely limited, forcing us to rely on reflexes to avoid collisions with the tunnel walls.

With no other vehicles in sight, we abandoned any notion of staying within a designated lane, instead using the cat's eye reflectors as rough guides to steer us through the murky darkness. Progress was slow, each kilometre feeling like an eternity as we made our way back to where we had started.

Near the tunnel entrance, a shadow of movement caught our eyes. Emerging from the darkness, a group of 5 men, led by a monk, approached with resolute strides. 2 of them, including the monk, were determined to walk out of the tunnel and leave the park behind. Without pausing for more than a brief greeting, they pressed forward on their path.

Among the others in the group, one limped heavily, bearing the visible wounds of the earthquake's wrath. The tale of their ordeal unfolded–a journey interrupted by the violent tremors bringing down landslides that left them battered and bruised. It was later revealed that they had been riding motorcycles when the earthquake struck, only to be thrown from their bikes by the force of falling rocks. Their injuries were evident–a broken elbow and ankle–painful reminders of their close brush with the calamity.

Monk walking through rubble towards the tunnel

Their arrival heralded the beginning of a stream of survivors, each with their own story of resilience in surviving the disaster. Among them, 2 women stood alongside 3 men, their faces etched with weariness but tinged with relief at their arrival into the tunnel. A tour guide in the group brought a glint of hope, as he could bridge the language divide with his fluent command of both English and Chinese.

Dust filled valley

More survivors follow

With communication barriers bridged, plans began to take shape as we grappled with our uncertain fate. As the hours passed, a realisation settled over us–the steady rainfall of rocks outside the tunnel served as a constant reminder of the dangers that lurked beyond the confines of our perimeter. With every aftershock that brought down landslides, the prospect of venturing out into the unknown grew increasingly dangerous.

Approximately an hour later, those who had initially planned to hike out of the tunnel emerged once again. They had congregated at the mouth of the tunnel, deliberating their next move. After observing for about half an hour, they noticed a continuous shower of rocks and stones descending at a steady rate. Recognising the danger, they unanimously agreed that it was too risky to proceed and retreated.

Now, with the afternoon waning into the evening, we resigned ourselves to our temporary shelter, clinging to hope despite the uncertainty. In the darkness of the tunnel, we waited, praying for the tremors to cease and the path to safety to reveal itself.

Bonds of Unity in the Tunnel of Uncertainty

3:00 PM

There was an urgency in the air. With 22 people sharing the confined space and limited resources, cooperation was going to be imperative. We needed to come together, to form a cohesive unit, and there was no time to waste. In that tunnel, with its dim lighting and dust-laden air, we gathered around, introducing ourselves, sharing stories of how we ended up there, trapped in the earthquake's aftermath.

Among the 22 individuals stranded in the tunnel, 6 of us spoke English, while the others primarily spoke Chinese with a smattering of English words. To protect the privacy of those involved, I will assign some of them fictitious names while capturing the essence of our group.

First, there was David—an American in his 50s. He was on a 2-month trip in Asia and found himself trapped on the trail of the Tunnel of Nine Turns while hiking when the earthquake struck. Despite sustaining injuries during the quake, he maintained a determined spirit. He captured a photo of the ordeal with a smile, ready to share his survival tale with loved ones back home. A storyteller and risk-taker, David meticulously calculated his options and advocated for evacuation, driven by the urgency of catching his flight the following day.

Then there was Chris, another American in his 50s, who was travelling outside the US for the first time. His kind smile, calm demeanour and optimism provided a comforting presence. Chris was with Bill, his tour guide, driving away from the Silks Place Hotel in Taroko when the earthquake hit. Fortunately, they were in a tunnel at the time. They ventured out to safety at the Lushui campsite. While the campsite remained intact, the surrounding trail had shown signs of damage.

Bill, the Taiwanese tour guide, emerged as our liaison to the outside world, bridging the language barrier with ease. He was driving the car with Chris, and together, they sought refuge in the tunnel when the earthquake struck. They abandoned the vehicle and walked to the Tunnel of Nine Turns in an attempt to journey out of the park. Bill was somewhat familiar with the terrain, and his resourcefulness proved invaluable as we navigated our escape options.

Alena, a spirited expat living in Singapore, was a seasoned hiker and a visitor to Taiwan for the long weekend. Her presence added a touch of resilience to our group. Despite the challenges we faced, her positive attitude inspired us to stay strong and hopeful. Caught off guard by the quake while starting a trail at Lushui, she joined forces with Chris and Bill, determined to hike their way out of Taroko.

Accompanied by 2 locals, Tao and Nan, who were on a bike and abandoned it to seek refuge in a tunnel when the earthquake struck, this group formed a crew of 5 and started their journey towards the Tunnel of Nine Turns, about 5 kilometres east of the Lushui trail, hoping to pass through and continue all the way out.

As we settled in for the afternoon, a humble guard room at the tunnel's entrance offered solace in the form of a steaming bowl of noodle soup. Despite the limited supply of food and utensils, we shared this simple meal with gratitude. Each person portioned a small amount of food for themself. After we ate, we'd wash and pass the cup & chopsticks to the next person in turn.

This was one of the moments that really stood out in the experience—a moment when humanity shone brightly as people showed up for one another with care and consideration. It was a reminder that even in the darkest of times, compassion and generosity have the power to unite us, offering hope and strength to face adversity together.

Through conversations about travel plans and the irony of our situation, we found time for light-hearted jokes about which celebrity would play each of us in the movie that would inevitably be made about the Hualien earthquake.

"When they make a movie about this, I want my character to be played by Scarlett Johansson," Alena declared, sparking laughter and agreement among us.

As for me, I couldn't help but nominate George Clooney to portray Gautam, perfectly capturing his charm and charisma.

Bound by Hope

3:45 PM

In the darkness of the tunnel, among the rubble and uncertainty, there was one shared desire among us all: to emerge from this ordeal alive. Each person's patience varied, influenced by their impending travel plans and flights out of Taipei. For some scheduled to depart on a Friday following the Wednesday morning earthquake, the intention was to trek out of the National Park and arrange private transportation to Taipei. Others, mainly locals, were divided in their urgency to leave; some sought immediate departure, while others opted to await rescue authority's intervention, deeming independent action too risky.

Gautam and I shared the wish to reunite with our families and inform them of our safety despite the coverage they may have seen in the news. In spite of Gautam's injury and the harrowing experience we had endured, we held on to the hope of soon reuniting with our loved ones to celebrate our second chance at life.

As evening descended, 3 locals–employees of the Silks Place Hotel in Taroko–resolved to brave the journey out. Familiar with the route as their daily commute, they decided to wager on the hotel's relative safety and ample supplies until rescue arrived. These very individuals had earlier cautioned against straying from the tunnel's safety. However, faced with dwindling rations amongst 20 occupants in the tunnel, a difficult choice loomed: to starve or risk being hit by rocks in landslides caused by aftershocks on the way out.

If this was to be our final chapter, the one thing we refused to surrender was our dignity–the dignity of not having to scramble for that last morsel of bread or sip of water. Thus, a group of 3, including Uri, the IT guy, decided to trek towards the hotel, 7 kilometres deeper into the National Park. This next action exemplifies the generosity of the Taiwanese people.

Despite facing a grave crisis with uncertain outcomes and no assurances of reaching safety themselves, Uri showed incredible compassion. He circulated a sheet of paper and a pen among the 20 individuals in the tunnel, inviting us to provide contact details for our loved ones. With a promise to personally inform our families of our safety, he initiated a chain of solidarity. This piece of paper became a symbol of hope, passed from hand to hand as if it were a sacred mission. Like soldiers, these men carried our messages to send word to our anxious families that we were safe.

We bid them farewell with prayers and encouragement as they stepped out of the tunnel and then disappeared around the bend, venturing into the unknown. Throughout the night, the rest of us remained huddled in the tunnel, hoping that the aftershocks would soon subside, and, with the dawn, clarity would emerge on our next course of action.

Contemplations at Sunset

5:30 PM

Before the last rays of daylight dwindled, Gautam and I ventured out for a brief stroll within the safety of the tunnel. Dust-stained figures surrounded us, some donning masks and helmets, others still in their hiking gear from the morning. In this makeshift environment, a fascinating ingenuity revealed itself as individuals improvised to adapt to the circumstances—either perched on a wooden bench or a makeshift cardboard mat. Luxuries like pillows, blankets, or mattresses were distant fantasies, and people from all backgrounds converged to find some quiet. If we were to emerge from this alive, we needed to recuperate from the day's ordeal and muster the strength to face the challenges of tomorrow.

Before settling in for the night, a group of us convened to strategise for the next day. We would remain united and attempt to walk out of the National Park on foot, bracing ourselves for the possibility of encountering landslides triggered by aftershocks. Despite setting out in the morning, we acknowledged the possibility of spending yet another night in the refuge of another tunnel along the way. With no communication with the outside world and the ceaseless rhythm of aftershocks, nothing was guaranteed.

As the sun set, Gautam and I sought solace in the relative comfort of our car. Reclining the seats, we made space for one more occupant in the backseat. As darkness enveloped the valley and the chill of night descended, Alena joined us in the car, and we nestled in, preparing to rest.

In the silence of the night, there was a cacophony of thoughts that reverberated within. Questions echoed incessantly: How did we find ourselves in this predicament? What stroke of fortune led us here? Will we emerge unscathed from this ordeal? Contemplations on whether to await rescue or take the gamble of venturing out into the unknown tormented me. Should we journey deeper into the National Park towards the Silks Place Hotel, or should we risk going in the opposite direction?

Paralysed by indecision, the only solace I found was in the reassuring presence of Gautam beside me. With one hand resting on his body, I whispered words of comfort into the darkness, anchoring myself in the knowledge that we were together, still breathing. "It's okay," I repeated softly, the words a mantra of reassurance. "We are okay. It's going to be okay. I love you. Good night."

Nightfall: Aftershocks and Inner Demons

7:30 PM

Our minds raced through a tumult of possibilities, from the best-case scenarios to the darkest outcomes, with the only predictable rhythm being the relentless cadence of aftershocks. Data from the Central Weather Association of Taiwan documented a staggering 25 aftershocks registering above a magnitude of 5 on the Richter scale—each one would have been classified as a separate earthquake had it not paled in comparison to the earlier 7.4 magnitude quake. These 25 substantial tremors were merely a fraction of the 446 aftershocks that besieged us during our time in the Tunnel of Nine Turns at Taroko National Park. Originating from depths ranging from 1 km to 50 km beneath our feet, each tremor brought upon us a cascade of landslides, sending stones tumbling and rocks clattering while stray metal fragments echoed their descent to the ground.

The onslaught was compounded by escalating winds coursing through the valley, carrying with them more debris of uprooted trees. The tunnel quivered under the force of the gusts, and the car trembled violently in response. Every movement within the car felt like a prelude to reliving the nightmare we so desperately sought to escape. My nerves were on high alert, my body primed for action, poised between fight and flight. My legs felt on fire, ready to run at a moment's notice—like a giant scarlet macaw trapped inside my belly, flapping its wings wildly, ready to take flight, creating jitters in my gut and generating spasms and cramps in every inch of my quads and calves.

At times, it felt as though I were trapped within my own body, yearning to break free. In those moments, my mind shut out the world, focused solely on surviving the present, minute by minute, second by second. Was this the essence of survival instinct? A mind prepared for the worst while clinging to hope for the best. In such circumstances, what recourse did we have but to pray and hope?

The air grew thick with dust, making each breath a struggle. As the night deepened, the cooler air seemed to amplify the density of the dust particles. Sleep eluded me, and I found myself compelled to step outside the car to stretch my cramped legs and ease the tension in my back.

A faint scent lingered in the air–beetroot. Was it hunger or delusion? The earthy aroma triggered memories of better times, of meals shared with loved ones. But now, it served as a reminder of the trauma we endured in the tunnel, threatening to overwhelm me once more. I stood on the precipice of despair, grappling with the ghosts of the past and the uncertainty of the future, yearning for escape from both the confines of the tunnel and the prison of my own mind.

Empty Belly, Overflowing Mind

9:00 PM - 5:00 AM (next day)

As hungry bellies churned with their respective thoughts, some resigned to sleep, while others delved into calculations of escape routes. Through the steady drumbeat of aftershocks, I sought solace in mindfulness, attempting to anchor myself in the present moment. Identifying thoughts as thoughts feelings as feelings, I focused on the rhythm of my breath, tuning my senses to the sounds echoing within the tunnel.

I drifted off, but sleep proved elusive. The car convulsed violently, jolting us awake. Another aftershock. As we stirred awake, reassurances were whispered in the darkness. "It's okay, I am here. We are still here. This will pass."

Stomachs rumble.

We shared the last of our rationed supplies, mindful of the need to conserve for the uncertain days ahead. On the positive side, with kilos of particle dust filling our eyes, ears, nose and mouths, it all tasted like mud anyway. We just needed to eat enough to sustain a little bit at a time.

The loop repeated in a relentless cycle as the night unfolded:

Thoughts>>Calculations>>Meditation>>Fleeting sleep>>Aftershocks.

Each wave of panic was met with whispered affirmations. "We're okay. We will get through this."

With the first light of dawn piercing through the gloom, the time for decision had arrived. Should we stay or attempt to leave? Which direction should we venture towards? Further into the National Park or in the opposite direction to get out?

We deliberated, weighing the options with a pros and cons assessment:

- **Stay back in the tunnel until rescued**
  - **Pros**
    - The tunnel offered stability and relative safety amidst the chaos.
    - We would likely survive until rescue arrives, albeit with dwindling supplies.
  - **Cons**
    - Limited water supplies would become depleted with a group of 20 people.
    - Uncertainty shrouded the timeline for rescue efforts, given the debris build-up on either side of the tunnel and continued aftershocks.
    - The anguish of our families weighed heavily on our minds.
    - Gautam's injury required medical attention or risked getting infected.

- **Attempt to leave the tunnel**
  - **Pros**
    - Higher likelihood of escaping the worst-hit area before rescue teams arrive.
    - Opportunity to procure medical aid for Gautam.
  - **Cons**
    - Blocked roads could trap us in another tunnel without supplies.
    - Risk of injury from aftershock-induced rockfall and landslides.
    - Treacherous hiking conditions through rubble and debris.

There was just not enough data to make a rational decision. In the end, it came down to gut instinct. We'd attempt to walk out, but brace for the risks ahead. It could pay off, but it could turn out to be a waste of valuable resources–water, food and our energy. There was only one way to find out. We had to try.

Now faced with 2 paths forward, we considered our options:

- **Towards The Silks Place Hotel, Taroko. 7 kilometres deeper into the National Park**

  o **Pros**
    - Familiarity with part of the route from previous attempts.
    - Potential access to food, water, and better first aid.
    - Possibility of utilising the hotel's parking lot as a helipad for emergency evacuation.

  o **Cons**
    - Aftershocks likely worsened trail conditions overnight.
    - Extended stay in the National Park increased vulnerability to weather and supply shortages.
    - I had not told him this so far, but Gautam was going to need stitches. We needed to get to a hospital ASAP.

- **Out of Taroko National Park, 15 kilometres to the Park Entrance**

  o **Pros**
    - Opportunity to contact family and seek urgent medical aid for Gautam.
    - Escape the hardest-hit area of Hualien and get to safety.

  o **Cons**
    - Longer distance to traverse through unknown terrain.
    - Increased risk of roadblocks and prolonged isolation.
    - Heightened danger of rockfall and landslides due to aftershocks.

Well, isn't that just great? The pros and cons assessment made it all crystal-clear. We now had an expected probability of success, and making the decision was a total walk in the park!

Except it was not.

None of this added up, and we were fully aware that both options would be a gamble. We did not even know if those brave souls who ventured out last evening made it to the hotel safely.

But fuelled by a primal need for food, water and basic hygiene as well as a desperate longing to reach our families, we reluctantly chose what seemed like the lesser evil. So, off we go, attempting to trek towards the Silks Place Hotel, Taroko, 7 kilometres deeper into the park.

It was a leap of faith, but something about that decision felt right.

No, scratch that. Something about that decision felt less wrong than the other options ahead of us.

The 'Talk'

5:15 AM on Thursday, 4-Apr 2024. (+1 day)

We have settled on a direction but deep down, I know this decision is just the tip of the iceberg. There are countless more choices looming ahead, and some will likely be even more daunting than the one we have just made.

Gautam and I huddle in the safety of the car, just the 2 of us, preparing for what lies ahead. I take the lead:

"Alright, let's lay it out. Here are the potential outcomes:

- We both make it to the Silks Place Hotel Taroko safely, OR
- We are forced to abandon the journey due to aftershocks and landslides, leaving us stranded in another tunnel further along.
- And then there are worse, more serious possibilities:
    - One of us sustains a serious injury, rendering us unable to continue on foot.
    - A massive landslide takes one of us into the gorge, or
    - We both meet a tragic end, slipping on loose rocks and falling into the gorge."

"Yes, any of these scenarios are possible," he responds, his demeanour calm and collected as always.

Every word I utter is a stark reality. These aren't exaggerated fears; they are the grim possibilities we face. We lock eyes, squeezing each other's hands in silent agreement. If tragedy strikes, the survivor will summon help for the other. It is a pact born of necessity, a commitment to push aside emotion until we are out of danger and reunited with our loved ones.

At that moment, I feel like a soldier bidding farewell to my comrade. I wish him well, hoping for the best while bracing for the worst. The past

24 hours have been gruelling, but there is still so much left to live for. Our lives will not be spoken of in the past tense just yet. We will fight for our survival.

Recalling this episode still brings a pang to my heart, but I am proud of us for having the talk. I am grateful we survived to share our story. Yet, if we had not made it out alive, my greatest regret would have been not having had this conversation.

If there is one lesson I have taken away from this experience, it is that we all face choices, and even deciding not to choose is a choice made. We could have dodged the tough conversation or remained in denial. But if tragedy had struck, there would be no turning back.

Leap of Faith

5:30 AM (+1 day)

We have made our decision. We are leaving the Tunnel of Nine Turns, heading deeper into the National Park towards the Silks Place Hotel, Taroko. It is a daunting 7-kilometre trek, and the entire path ahead is unfamiliar. The aftermath of the landslides has left the roads strewn with debris–rocks, stones, twigs, and dust–creating varying degrees of obstacles along the route. Some sections resemble craters, while others are buried beneath mountains of rubble. We will need to tread carefully.

I am still uncertain if this is the right choice, but I defer to Gautam to decide for both of us. I am on the verge of tears, overwhelmed by fatigue, hunger and the stress of our situation. I need to let it all out; I need to cry. I need to be able to wail and grieve at the situation. I want to sob openly, but I know I must remain composed. We have a long journey ahead of us, and breaking down now is not an option. I have to muster strength–for myself, for Gautam, for our families. I am ready to take a leap of faith.

I allow myself a moment to shed a few tears, offer a silent prayer, and then give Gautam a tight hug–the second tightest we've shared in the past 24 hours. The tightest was during the earthquake itself, when fear gripped us, as rocks rained down and we faced our death.

He gives me a bit of a pep talk: "It's fine, this is going to be easy. You've got this, you've been training for this. You are strong–physically and mentally." He knows what I need to hear.

"All right," I responded, mustering resolve. "Let's do this. I love you."

We huddle with the group and develop a strategy. The group has 10 people - 6 tourists who speak English and 4 locals who primarily speak Chinese. We agree to split into 2 groups of 5 each and maintain a 'safe distance' between the groups to budget for a suitable amount of space–space to allow for potential hazards.

The reality of the situation was that rocks could fall, anyone could slip if caught in an aftershock while trying to cross a particularly treacherous section of the trail, or someone could get seriously injured. We needed to hedge, and we needed to be prepared for fatalities, among other mishaps.

With nods of agreement, the group exchanged determined glances. There were no words of luck or encouragement–none were needed. We understood the risks and were prepared to face them head-on.

Before we departed from the tunnel, I approached Alice and Ying, the 2 Silks Place Hotel employees who had offered us assistance after the earthquake. I informed them of our decision to leave.

"You're leaving? But it is still not safe out there," Alice remarked, her concern evident.

"We are a group of 10," I replied, gesturing towards the group of people standing together. "We are going to try to reach the hotel."

Alice and Ying shared a sombre look and shrugged. They declined the offer to join us, opting to wait for rescue teams instead. They deemed walking out too unsafe. However, they did make a request.

"If you are leaving, could you leave your car open for us to spend the night?" Alice asked.

The car, a rental, was trivial in comparison to the safety of people. We would deal with the consequences of an abandoned rental car later. But for now, leaving it behind was the only option. Lives were at stake, and our priorities were clear.

Of course, we were going to leave the car behind, offering it as shelter for those who remained. Of course, we would leave it open for anyone to stay warm through the night. It was a small gesture, but in times like these, every act of kindness counts.

PART 4

The Dangerous Walk to Safety

Gearing up for the Journey

Before we set out on our journey, I assess what essentials we will need to bring along. We have to be prepared for the possibility of spending another night in a tunnel along the way. Water, a bar of candy, pain relief medicines, our caps–those are the basics. And then there is my trusty chapstick–I never leave home without it, and this situation is no exception. I stash it in my back pocket, ready for the journey ahead.

Thankfully, I also found my ankle brace in the car, along with a knee brace for Gautam. My ankle, with 2 busted ligaments, is prone to instability, while Gautam's knee injury calls for extra support. Though we did not anticipate needing them for the earlier trail on the Tunnel of Nine Turns, having the braces with us provided a much-needed sense of security, bolstering our confidence in our ability to make the journey.

I searched through the car for any additional supplies, but came up empty-handed in terms of first aid. However, I did find a reflective vest–a potentially life-saving discovery. In case of serious injury, the vest could help rescuers locate us more easily. It is a small detail, but in survival mode, every precaution counts. I don the vest, mindful of the need to ration weight in our backpacks.

Scouring the boot for something that could serve as a helmet yielded no results. Just the usual equipment to change a flat tyre along with rubber matting and felt carpets–nothing to keep our heads safe from falling stones. Instead, I borrowed a spare cap from a fellow hiker, and padded it with some clothing for makeshift protection against falling stones. Gautam opted for a cap and a jacket, keeping it simple yet practical.

With one small backpack and a tote bag carrying food supplies, we pack strategically. The essentials–phones, wallet, keys, water, and a protein bar–go in the backpack, leaving hands free for manoeuvrability through rough trail surfaces. Especially if we needed all limbs to climb over rubble like a mountain goat. The tote holds other items that we are prepared to abandon, if necessary. Life takes precedence over possessions.

We bid farewell to those staying behind in the tunnel, and I took a picture of the last known location of the car in the tunnel, in case we needed to share it with the rental company.

Alice offered us spare masks to protect against the dust. "God bless you, good luck," she said, adding a piece of advice: "Stay close to the mountain."

With gratitude and well-wishes exchanged, we split into 2 groups as planned, ready to embark on the journey ahead. And so, it begins.

Last known location of the car before we set out

The only visible section of the trail from the tunnel

Stay Close to the Mountain

5:46 AM (+1 day)

The first few steps away from the shelter of the tunnel are terrifying. The once scenic road, flanked by majestic mountains and a flowing river, now resembles a scene from a post-apocalyptic movie. Debris litters the path, a reminder of the destructive potential of the earthquake and following aftershocks.

"Stay close to the mountain," they advised. A simple rule grounded in logic–the mountain provides a buffer against falling rocks and debris. Rocks driven by landslides would bounce along the mountain, making them more likely to fall away from the mountain face. But in this unpredictable terrain, nothing is guaranteed. We proceed cautiously, keeping watch for any signs of danger.

This first kilometre is treacherous, the path is flooded with stones, rock and debris, with the constant threat of tremors and landslides hanging over us. My ankle brace provides some stability, but the uneven ground demands intense concentration. Each step feels like a battle against the odds.

Debris littered the path

Like a scene from a post-apocalyptic
movie scene

Paranoia sets in, as my mind conjures up scenes from apocalyptic movies. Every possibility feels all too real as we trudge through the debris. I cannot shake the fear of injury–stray metal piercing my flesh, wood shrapnel tearing through my skin. It is a gruesome mental minefield.

I can't help but think of the human dynamics portrayed in the movies. The initial solidarity gives way to self-preservation, as resources dwindle and injuries mount. Inevitably, my mind goes to thoughts about where I would fit into that narrative–whether I'd be deemed 'weak' and left behind. But with Gautam by my side, I find a different kind of strength.

He is a source of strength and reassurance. His calm demeanour balances my anxiety and his words of encouragement keep me going. Together, we manoeuvre the treacherous terrain, leaning on each other for support. He keeps his head up, turning around every few minutes to check in with me. I try to stay as close to him as possible, but he is adapting to the terrain faster than I can.

Trees uprooted, fallen branches, twigs and leaves add to the debris

Debris rolled over into tunnels

We round a corner, after which the mouth of the tunnel disappears from view. There is no turning back now. I press on, one foot in front of the other, determined to see this journey through. In those first few minutes, I experience a strange mix of emotions–calm and control, interspersed with moments of panic. But adrenaline courses through my veins, fuelling progress and masking the pain. It provides the burst of energy we need to persevere through the journey ahead.

The human mind's capacity to adapt never ceases to amaze me. While operating in survival mode, it developed a special 'battery saver' setting, shutting down non-essential functions to conserve energy for the essentials. Despite cramping legs, a jittery stomach, and a chest-pounding with adrenaline, our minds remained focused on the task at hand–to keep moving forward, one step at a time.

Our group, consisting of 3 English speakers–Gautam, myself and Alena–and a local couple, Tao and Nan, formed the first of 2 teams. The others, who had ventured partway on the hike the previous day, joined the second group. Tao and Nan, being natives of Taroko, brought invaluable knowledge of the terrain, navigating the landscape with skill and precision.

Their partnership was seamless, each one complementing the other's strengths. In particularly risky sections prone to landslides, one of them would hang back as a lookout. If the path was deemed safe, they'd signal the rest of us with a series of urgent "GO GO GO GO GO" calls, prompting us to move quickly through the danger zone.

We relied on their expertise and quick thinking, grateful for their presence as we forged ahead into the unknown.

Hikers on a devastated path

Once clear roads, now carpeted with a layer of dust and constant risk of landslides

Observations of the Terrain

6:00 AM (+1 day)

As we embarked on our journey through the rugged terrain, the landscape unfolded before us in a series of striking scenes, etching itself into my memory:

- First, the sight of clouds of dust billowing out from the mountains, resembling wisps of smoke rising into the sky. It was a surreal sight, a reminder of the seismic activity that had reshaped the landscape around us.
- As we ventured further, the dust had settled, blanketing the roads in a thick layer of fine particles. What was once a clean road surface, had transformed into a dusty carpet, marking the passage of our footsteps through the tunnels.
- Alongside the road, remnants of the quake lay strewn haphazardly. Uprooted trees, broken branches, and scattered leaves mingled with the rubble of rocks, bricks, stones, and twisted metal.
- Abandoned vehicles, their tyres deflated, and frames battered, stood as silent witnesses to the chaos that had unfolded.

Clouds of dust billowed out from the mountains

Dust blanketed roads in a thick carpet of fine particles with footsteps imprinted

Remnants of the quake lay strewn haphazardly. Uprooted trees, broken branches, and scattered leaves mingled with the rubble of rocks, bricks, stones and twisted metal

Abandoned vehicles, their tyres deflated, and frames battered, stood as silent witnesses to the chaos

Dust flooded the valley like smoke rising into the sky, making each breath difficult

Through this scene of destruction, we manoeuvred a terrain fraught with more danger and uncertainty than we had anticipated. Each step required careful consideration–from rocky slopes to narrow paths bordered by sheer cliffs, we understood that we would need to adapt our approach to minimise the risk posed by the ever-changing terrain.

1. A trail flanked by a vertical mountain face: In the event of aftershocks triggering landslides, proximity to the mountain offers the best refuge. Should rocks cascade down the slope, they are prone to ricochet off the mountain and land on the opposite side of the path. Thus, sticking close to the mountain provides a measure of safety. We tread cautiously, one hand almost grazing the mountain, while debris gathered on the far side of the trail.

AI-generated image of a vertical mountain face with a road carved out

Real image of the terrain

2. Path with a sloping mountain face: In the event that an aftershock causes a landslide, safety is elusive. Stray rocks, propelled by momentum, offer no refuge; they hurtle relentlessly, posing a direct threat of injury or, worse, sending unsuspecting hikers into the gaping gorge below. Survival demands swift action–an instinctual sprint across the treacherous terrain. The sole recourse is to rely on intuition and push forward. There is no looking back; only a desperate race to reach safety before the next aftershock triggers another cascade of debris. Every step is a gamble, praying that the restless tectonic plates grant safe passage.

AI-generated image of a sloping mountain face with a road carved out

Real image of the terrain with large stones and rocks from the landslide

3. Path covered by the mountain. This type of enclave served as a 'safety stop', covered by the mountain's overhead shield, deterring stray rocks. These sections typically afford respite, allowing for a momentary slowdown, a sip of water, and a pause to regroup before continuing the journey.

AI-generated image of a road protected
by the mountain overhang

Actual image of path protected from
landslides

Within just the initial kilometre of our hike, we had encountered all 3 landscapes, but I had no idea what awaited ahead.

The Impossible Mound

6:20 AM (+1 day)

About 15 to 20 minutes into our journey along the rugged trail, our progress had been steady despite the bumpy terrain beneath our feet. We had not encountered any aftershocks since emerging from the tunnel–a fact that initially seemed reassuring. However, as we rounded yet another bend in the path, our optimism waned as we faced the site ahead.

A massive landslide had cascaded down the sloping face of the mountain, creating a chaotic collage against its 70-degree incline. The debris, comprising rocks, stones, twigs, trees, assorted metal and rubber wreckage, ensnared within a haze of settling dust, had accumulated into a mound stretching at least 60 feet along the road.

This mound rose at a precarious 45-degree angle against the mountain. The only feasible route lay in ascending and descending this barrier, relying solely on scant protrusions of stray rocks and twigs for support. On our right lay the looming threat of the landslide-prone mountain, while to the left yawned a dizzying 50-storey plunge into the gaping gorge.

Massive landslide accumulated into a mound, stretching 60 feet along the road at a 45-degree angle against the mountain

Chaotic collage of rocks, stones, twigs, trees, assorted metal and rubber wreckage, ensnared within a haze of settling dust

Standing there, one could not help but muse that encountering tremors earlier might have been less treacherous than if an aftershock sprang up now, as we were trying to cross this section. This segment of the trail was undeniably the most dangerous, where the slightest misstep could mean doom. With each passing minute, the possibility of an imminent aftershock loomed, promising to either augment the mound with debris or, worse, send us hurtling into the abyss.

But retreat was not an option; onward was our sole recourse. Gautam assumed the lead, surging ahead with resolve. Almost instinctively, he ascended the mound and I followed suit, grappling with uncertainty as I sought stable footing in the unsteady terrain. Each step demanded a cautious double-check to ensure the rock would hold steady with my weight. My legs quivered, compelling me to resort to all fours for stability.

Limbs pressed against stone, fingers clawing at the mountain's facade, I contorted my body at odd angles, navigating what felt like a vertical ascent in certain spots. My tote bag, carrying food and water, now transformed into a hindrance. Then, in a moment of fatal distraction, I stole a glance upward at the sheer mountain face, only to be confronted by the gaping maw of the gorge below.

Looming threat of the landslide-prone mountain on our right, and a 50-storey plunge into the gaping gorge on our left

Note: Credit for these images goes to our fellow hikers in group 2. There is a unique bond that forms when people share an experience as intense as this. I have stayed in touch with many of the others who braved through it with us. We've been exchanging messages and checking in on each other's progress. Some are gradually finding their way back to a sense of normalcy, while others, me included, are still navigating the aftermath. Chen, the road construction worker, snapped this photo and shared it a few days post-ordeal.

Terror seized me, eclipsing even the horror of the earthquake itself, as a wave of emotions flooded my consciousness—grief, anxiety, gratitude, love, and anger—all converging in a tumultuous whirlwind of despair.

In that instant, on the brink of surrender, I faltered, my grip slipping as the ground threatened to give way beneath me. With a surge of panic, I resigned myself to the inevitability of my fate, grappling with the crushing weight of regret for having embarked upon this journey of my own volition.

"I don't think I can do this," I confessed, my voice trembling with uncertainty. "It is too loose; I cannot hold on. I am going to slip." He could see I was struggling.

"You've got this. It's almost over. Just step on that stone, and then you can slide down," Gautam reassured. He had reached the other side and had stopped to wait for me.

My mouth was dry, my brain in overdrive, my eyes frenzied, and my palms sweating. There, in the throes of despair, a flicker of determination ignited within me. I resolved to seize control of my own destiny. Casting aside the burden of my tote bag, I took one step forward, spurred on by Gautam's encouragement echoing in my ears.

Summoning reserves of strength I never knew I possessed, I took 2 more vertical steps—each one a leap of faith. Miraculously, the rocks held firm beneath my weight, propelling me to the top of the mound.

From there, the descent was swift—a chaotic blur of sliding rubble as I reunited with Gautam. No words were exchanged, but the shared relief spoke volumes. Together, we continued along the path until we reached a safer spot, where we awaited the group's arrival.

Later, I will reflect on this decision—the delicate balance between fear and resilience, between life and the abyss.

Rest Between Sprints

6:43 AM (+1 day)

The worst was behind us. The stretches of road ahead appeared longer, though still undulated. Yet, in comparison to the impossible mound, these patches posed no more than 80% of the difficulty. It felt almost effortless now, knowing that we had braved through the worst. Debris still littered the way, necessitating occasional climbs, but the cliffs were gentler. We had traversed the deepest part of the gorge, and the mountains were gradually parting ways, leading us towards flatter terrain–the valley nestled between the peaks.

Here, among the remnants of landslides, we manoeuvred our way to the 'safer' sections of the trail. These segments were either sheltered by the mountain overhead, covered by tunnels, or on a bridge connecting 2 peaks. Remarkably, they retained their form and function despite the relentless quakes.

Stray rocks viewed from the bridge

Size of stones compared to a person

Our strategy was to move swiftly and sprint when confronted with rubble along the path–those sections were the most susceptible to further landslides. Conversely, we slowed our pace to conserve energy on clear stretches. If the road had not suffered significant damage during the initial quake, aftershocks were less likely to wreak havoc. The locals among us kept a vigilant watch, offering warnings in precarious stretches, their guidance proving invaluable.

7:00 AM We paused at a bridge for a much-needed hydration break, waiting for our companions from group #2 to catch up. To my astonishment, Chris appeared, bearing my abandoned tote bag from the impossible mound. His act of kindness warmed my heart–an unexpected gesture that spoke volumes about the bond that had formed in the group during a time of adversity. The contents of the bag–a can of Pringles and a snicker bar–belonged to him, yet he gave them up without hesitation. I felt undeserving of his generosity.

Hydration rest-stop at a bridge where you can see me wearing the reflective vest, ankle brace and using a stray twig as a hiking stick

Massive boulders brought down to the road by landslides

As the others congregated at the bridge, we took a brief stop for check-ins and hydration.

"Is everyone okay?"

"As okay as can be, given the circumstances. Everyone is still breathing and walking. That's a win."

And so, we resumed the journey. 15 minutes ahead, signs of civilisation emerged–a campsite! A family of 3 roamed about, their cars parked in a nearby lot, their son munching on rice crisps. They appeared unscathed and oddly pristine, compared to our bedraggled group, with mud-streaked clothes, dust-caked masks, and caps concealing weary faces. I still wore the reflective vest, and a twig had become my makeshift hiking stick.

Though they conversed in Chinese, I gleaned the essence of the conversation.

"Where are you coming from?" the lady at the campsite queried.

"From the Tunnel of Nine Turns," one of our group members replied.

"How are things there? Are there others?"

"It has been rough, but there are people. Some are injured," came the response.

"Where are you headed?"

"We are aiming for the Silks Place Hotel in Taroko for access to supplies."

"Are you sure it is safe? We've found relative safety here at the campsite. Our cars are parked."

Indeed, their vehicles stood unscathed, and tents dotted the area, their occupants seemingly making the most of an unexpected mountain retreat. They extended an invitation for us to utilise the campsite facilities–showers and toilets–where we washed away the dust from the impossible mound and took a moment to regroup. After fuelling our hunger with a quick snack, we bid the campers farewell and continued onward.

The Final Stretch

7:35 AM (+1 day)

For another 20 minutes, we trudged along, the once formidable distance between the mountains now widening. The dust had begun to settle, signalling a semblance of respite. The landscape appeared less apocalyptic than the harrowing sights we had encountered earlier. Though scattered with massive rocks and boulders around the campsites, the overall state seemed comparatively tame.

Navigating a few remaining patches of debris, we continued onward despite the persistent ache in our muscles, the gnawing hunger, thirst, and fatigue. Yet, with each step, the burden seemed lighter, the ordeal more manageable. We stumbled upon a lush green, open campsite–the starting point of the Lushui trail–an oasis in the chaos.

The campsite boasted a parking lot with cars, quaint sitting areas, a charming deck and essential amenities–a welcome change from the wilderness we had traversed over the past few hours. And then, a rare luxury we had not encountered in what felt like an eternity–a telephone booth! With renewed hope, we approached the phone booth, eager to make contact with our families.

Alas, the phone could only dial the local police–a small comfort, yet a lifeline, nonetheless. Bill seized the opportunity, relaying vital information to the authorities about our predicament and the whereabouts of others still stranded in the Tunnel of Nine Turns.

Though the trail had eased, the fear of uncertainty loomed large. The roads to the east, leading out of Taroko National Park, remained impassable, prolonging our ordeal. Although we were nearing our destination, the Silks Place Hotel, we braced ourselves to spend several nights camped at the hotel, aware that medical attention for Gautam was still a distant hope.

With a moment's respite, we turned inward, checking in with each other.

"How are you feeling? Does it hurt?" I asked.

"Not really. It's strange," Gautam replied, masking his pain. "How bad is it?"

We peeled back the dressing, revealing the extent of his injury–a deep, raw wound exposing layers of flesh on his cheek. The severity of it struck me: I know he is going to need stitches. We cannot wait too long. Yet Gautam remained unflinching–not a tear nor a single complaint.

From a distance, I heard Alena's voice, "Neil!"

Her voice carried across the campsite, drawing our attention to a familiar figure–a friend from the previous day. It dawned on me that this was the very campsite from where some members of our group had embarked on their ill-fated journey, trekking to the Tunnel of Nine Turns, only to find themselves stranded overnight before retracing their steps in a bid to reach safety.

At the time, unaware of the extent of the devastation, they had made their choices based on the information available. Life, it seemed, had a way of revealing its complexities only in hindsight.

Neil, who was camping at this site, had a car at his disposal. He offered us a fresh set of first-aid supplies–clean cotton and saline to irrigate a wound, antiseptic ointment and gauze. As I tended to Gautam's injury, his pain palpable with each touch, I could not help but marvel at his resilience. With a wry smirk, he examined his wound through the lens of my phone's camera and simply exclaimed, "Wow, that is pretty bad! Quite the adventure we've had."

8:10 AM In the relative safety of the campsite, we felt the earth tremble once more. We exchanged wary glances, confirming our shared experience–an aftershock striking just as we sought refuge around a stone table in the sun? How fortunate we were, I mused, to have experienced our first aftershock within the safety of this sanctuary. It could have come anywhere along the trail, but destiny had determined our time just wasn't up yet.

The group had dispersed around the campsite. With the tremors, everyone gathered around the parking area and agreed it was time to keep moving. Neil offered to drive us to the hotel.

"There's a short patch of road and then a long tunnel and a final stretch until the hotel," he said. "I have taken a couple of people earlier, and the car won't go all the way to the hotel, but it won't be a long walk." He kindly offered to take the bags and ferry the injured.

Alena, Gautam, and I got in the car with Neil. A 10-minute drive later, he had navigated the hurdles on the terrain, guiding us through tunnels and past obstacles with expert precision. We were now standing outside the gates of the Silks Place Hotel, Taroko...

PART 5

Respite and Recovery

From a Dystopian Reality

8:30 AM (+1 day)

Emerging from the Tianxiang Tunnel, we crossed the Zhihui Bridge into Tianxiang Square–a stark contrast to the desolate landscape we had seen over the past 24 hours. The scene before us felt surreal, like stepping into a different world altogether. Squeaky clean tourists strolled around, children laughed, and the air was filled with the buzz of excitement. Staff were in uniforms and tourists carried cameras around their necks. A pleasant smell filled the air, as people wearing hats and sunglasses walked about, smelling of perfume.

Alena, Gautam, and I stumbled into the lobby of the luxurious five-star hotel, feeling like refugees seeking asylum. Covered in blood, dust, and grime from our treacherous journey, we must have looked like ghosts walking into the space with polished marble floors, wood-panelled ceilings, and opulent furnishings. The stares of the clean, well-dressed guests bore into us, their curiosity evident. Who were these bedraggled travellers, and from where had they come?

Famished and fatigued, parched and pale, I was still wearing the reflective vest, my ankle brace and double cap. Alena had her helmet on, and Gautam had one hand on his face to keep the bandage in place. I felt like a zombie. As curious stares followed us, I couldn't help but feel a pang of self-consciousness–were we really so out of place here?

We walked to the hotel reception, where the kindest staff greeted us.

"Are you okay? Where are you coming from?" They asked, offering us bottles of water.

Accepting the water gratefully, we explained our ordeal, assuring them that, though shaken, we were physically unharmed. We had made it out of the nightmare. I asked if we could make a call to an international number. They passed me a pen and a piece of paper.

8:42 AM (+1 day)

With a shaky voice and trembling hands, I wrote down my father's number. The lady behind the desk dialled and handed me the phone. As I heard the dial tone, I could feel the emotions rising from my chest to my throat. I grabbed some tissues from the desk; I knew it was all about to come out. I had held it together for too long.

I heard my father's voice on the phone. "Hello?"

"Papa, it's me," I choked out before dissolving into tears. At that moment, the floodgates opened, releasing the pent-up fear, relief, and gratitude that had been building inside me. I was uncontrollable, inconsolable.

I did not think I was going to make it to hear his voice again. Mom came on speakerphone.

Through sobs and sniffles, I found my voice again to continue, "We are okay. We are alright. We made it. We were on the trail when the earthquake struck, but I am fine; Gautam is fine. He got a little hurt, but he is okay. It has been a nightmare, but we have reached a hotel, and I am calling you from their reception. It is safe here."

I wanted to tell them everything. Where we were when it happened, how we spent the night in a tunnel, holed up in a car, how we hiked to the hotel and how lucky we were to still be here–alive. I don't know how much I told them on that call, or how long we spoke, before Gautam nudged me to hurry up. There were other people waiting to make calls.

I was crying; my parents were crying. I could hear the relief in their voices. I could finally feel a wave of relief flood my entire body. For the first time in a long time, I told my parents I loved them. I was in such disbelief that we had made it to see another day. To hear my family's voice again.

They wanted to speak to Gautam–to hear his voice. He was calm and collected, as always. He told them, "All is well. I got a little hurt, but I will be fine."

He did the responsible thing and told my parents to contact his family and let them know we were fine. In just 24 hours, we had gotten accustomed to prudence with resources. Making an international call, even from a five-star hotel lobby, should be considered a precious resource.

We gave our families the hotel's phone number and let them know that mobile reception was still unstable, as cell towers were damaged with the earthquake. We told them we would get in touch when we could.

"We are okay, we will try to map out next steps and keep you posted. I love you."

The hotel receptionist, moved by our emotional exchange, inquired about our ordeal, her eyes brimming with tears, as we recounted our journey from the Tunnel of Nine Turns. Eager to know the fate of her colleagues, she asked how many were with us and how they fared. I shared the names of some of the other individuals and showed a few photos to reassure her that they were safe, albeit unable to accompany us on the hike. Upon hearing this news, her relief was palpable, and she exhaled joy as she learned of her colleagues' safety.

To a State of Utopia

9:00 AM (+1 day)

Sensing our distress, the receptionist brought out a first-aid kit. It was a marvel to behold–the largest and most well-stocked kit we had encountered thus far. With its ample supplies, we could finally tend to Gautam's wound properly, no longer relying on makeshift solutions. Selecting the necessary items from the kit: saline, antiseptic, cotton, gauze, and medical tape, we set to work. The hotel staff also offered pain medication, though adrenaline still coursed through our veins, numbing the ache for the time being.

Our inquiries about a room were met with the reality of a fully occupied hotel, its guests now confined within its walls due to the earthquake. Despite this, the hospitality extended to us was abundant. Access to communal facilities–bathrooms, showers, the café, and amenities– was generously offered, along with an invitation to indulge in buffet breakfast & lunch until 1 PM. Self-service laundry facilities stood ready for use in the basement, along with amenity trolleys parked around the lobby for people to help themselves.

A toothbrush! I grabbed 2 kits along with some cotton pads and earbuds. Our first stop was the restrooms, where we tended to Gautam's wounds, amongst curious gazes of other hotel guests who ventured in to inquire about our situation.

"What happened to Gautam? What was it like outside? What had we been through to get here?" Gautam, with his bandage, was like a star attraction.

Photo taken in the restroom after cleaning out
dirt and dried blood from the wound shows
how deep the lacerations are

We entertained a few questions before making our way to get some rest. We were not particularly hungry, but the restless energy pulsing through our brains made any attempts to sleep seem futile. As we found ourselves gravitating towards the dining area for breakfast, we were confronted by the wait staff, who asked for our room number.

"Umm, we are earthquake refugees?" I offered with a shrug. "The receptionist directed us here for breakfast." And just like that, without hesitation, they ushered us in, securing us a table among the morning bustle.

The scene that greeted us felt like something out of a utopia. After the apocalyptic journey we had endured, the sight of a breakfast buffet laden with salads, cold cuts, cheeses, pastries, yoghurt, fruits, breads, and savoury treats felt unreal. Adding to the atmosphere was soft jazz playing in the background while people sat leisurely around tables, sipping orange juice or tea and coffee in the morning sun.

Incredible. I had to pinch myself to believe it. Was this reality? Or had everything we experienced in the past 25 hours been just a nightmare? We looked around in disbelief, our senses in a tizzy as we adjusted to this new world. Finally, switching on our phones, we attempted to find network reception–without success.

Still lacking appetite, I filled my plate with eggs, vegetables, and a bun labelled 'Black sesame bun, Taiwan speciality.' But first, a cup of tea. As I made my way to the beverage station, a peculiar sight arrested my attention–an entire gelato bar. Gelato. At breakfast? It was enough to induce another moment of disbelief, gratitude, and relief. Here we were, still alive to witness another day and taste another flavour of gelato. I sipped my tea, savoured the surroundings, and marvelled at our good fortune.

I had this urge to eat more, as if my brain believed I needed to stockpile reserves for whatever other calamities lay ahead. Yet, my body refused to comply. Deciding to save a slice of chocolate cake for later, I grabbed a cup of coffee to go, all the while marvelling at how everyone around me continued about their day as if nothing had changed. After all we had been through, I was itching to talk to someone and tell the story.

I bumped into a kind-looking lady at the coffee machine.

"Hi, I'm Nam. How have things been here since the earthquake? It seems surprisingly peaceful," I inquired.

"I'm Claire," she responded in an Irish accent, "We were having breakfast when the earthquake hit. People rushed outside, but fortunately, the hotel structure remained intact, although some furnishings and pieces of cutlery rattled. So, most of us found safety within the hotel."

"It has been a nightmare in the National Park," I blurted out, the words pouring forth as if a dam had burst. "We were on a trail when the earthquake struck and ended up trapped in a tunnel all night."

I launched into the tale, taken over by an overwhelming need to share the ordeal. It is as if recounting it over and over again was the only way to convince myself that it was not just a terrible dream. "We just completed a harrowing hike to make it here."

"The hotel staff has been incredibly kind, and we are grateful to be alive," I continued, the words rushing out in a torrent of relief and gratitude. "They've opened their facilities to us so we can rest and reach out to our families."

"I am so sorry you had to endure such a nightmare," Claire offered sympathetically. "If there is anything you need, please don't hesitate to ask. We are staying on the 3rd floor of this hotel," she added, providing me with their room number. "If you need a place to rest, our room is open to you."

'Wow, that is extremely generous,' I thought. We barely just met, and I looked like crap, and yet a stranger offered me her bed to sleep in. People can be really kind!

It is amazing how kindness can shine through, even in the most unexpected moments. Despite just meeting and feeling less than our best, a stranger extended a generous gesture by offering their bed for a good rest. It is a reminder that compassion needs no bounds, and that simple acts of kindness can make a big difference. In a world where rushing and individualism prevail, encountering such genuine generosity was truly heartwarming.

Initially, I hesitated to accept her generous offer, feeling that it might be imposing. However, as I continued to ramble about our plans to use the self-service laundry, Claire surprised me with another gesture of kindness.

"Would you like a fresh change of clothes while you're washing yours? My husband can spare something for yours if you would like," she offered warmly.

The thought about what we would wear during the laundry process had not even crossed my mind. A bathrobe seemed like the only option, but the idea of wearing actual clothes was unexpectedly comforting.

And so, a simple act of sharing clothes marked the beginning of a friendship with Claire and her husband, Gearóid, during our stay at Taroko's Silks Place Hotel.

Oasis of Luxury

10:30 AM (+1 day)

The Silks Place Hotel stood as a sanctuary, its generosity extending beyond the confines of its booked rooms. They graciously extended the use of their common facilities and offered us every amenity afforded to resident guests.

In the lobby, we waited, surrounded by an air of tranquility. Hotel guests emerged from their rooms, freshly showered and satiated from breakfast, their bellies content. Some sought guidance from the concierge, inquiring about nearby trails for exploration or seeking recommendations for activities.

Internally, I wrestled the urge to scream—to caution them against venturing beyond the safety of the hotel walls. It seemed foolish to risk the dangers lurking outside, where tremors continued, and rocks threatened to fall. How could people be so oblivious? But before I could voice my concerns, the composed hotel staff intervened, delicately advising against exploration while rescue efforts were underway.

Following the earthquake, most guests of the Silks Place Hotel found themselves cut off from the outside world, deprived of television, news, and the internet. Aside from this, however, the hotel functioned seamlessly, offering electricity, hot water, and a plethora of amenities—a business centre with a beautiful view of the river flowing through the mountains, a massive banquet hall and a play area for children.

From the café to the gym, the indoor pool with its accompanying Jacuzzis to the rooftop outdoor pool with sun loungers offering breathtaking views, the Silks Place Hotel remained an oasis of comfort and luxury. Among these offerings, perhaps the most whimsical was the children's pool, adorned with an impressive array of 5,000 floating rubber ducks—a sight to behold.

Claire and Gearóid brought us 3 sets of clothes each—for us to choose from! 'How incredibly generous,' I thought.

I picked a red racerback, a pair of track pants and a jumper. Gautam picked a pair of shorts and a T-shirt. The receptionist pointed us in the direction of the indoor pool, located in the basement, where we could use the common shower facilities. We left our shoes outside and tip-toed inside, ashamed of our own condition—our feet still covered in dust, hair filled with dirt and clothes filthy from the hike.

I picked up a fresh towel and latched the door inside the shower cubicle. Even before I could turn on the shower, I felt the water come down my face. My tears flowed, mixed with the dirt from my face. It was eventually washed away by fragrant body wash, shampoo and conditioner. Feeling like I was born again, I changed into clean clothes to meet Gautam and Alena outside.

We collected the pile of dirty clothes for laundry. Armed with single-use slippers from the hotel reception to replace our worn 'earthquake shoes,' we walked out into the hotel corridors with newfound freedom.

The first signs of mobile reception started to come in. We were finally able to make some calls back home, albeit on very flaky connectivity. Families, relieved to hear our voices, remained anxious. Now keen to do everything in their capacity to help us, they were activating networks, getting in touch with people they knew in Taiwan and connecting with embassies with a focus on getting us out ASAP, so Gautam could get the medical attention he needed, and we could get back home safely, soon.

Inundated with calls and messages, the weight of responsibility grew heavier. Prioritising communication with immediate family, I grappled with the limitations of our situation. Yet, the connections unlocked brought so much peace, reminding us that through the darkest of times, we were not alone.

First News from the Outside World

11:30 AM (+1 day)

We roamed the corridors of the hotel, looking for a quiet place to rest. Along the way, we bumped into people who were keen to help in any way they could. Within the first few hours, we had access to most things we needed –

- Chargers for our phones.
- Medicines and antibiotics.
- An Apple watch charger–even in the aftermath of a massive earthquake, tracking our step count seemed oddly incongruent, yet necessary.

However, it was the influx of information that proved most invaluable. As sporadic connectivity came back to life, fragmented messages from the outside world began to trickle in, painting a picture of the devastation wrought by the earthquake.

The epicentre, a mere 10 kilometres from our location in Hualien, had unleashed a seismic force of 7.4 magnitude. It was a shallow quake, occurring just 15 kilometres beneath the surface, whose impact reverberated most fiercely through Taroko National Park. Landslides had ravaged the landscape, leaving hundreds stranded amidst the wreckage, with reports of collapsed buildings, impassable roads, and tragic loss of life.

- Authorities had confirmed 4 fatalities in Hualien County following a severe magnitude 7.4 earthquake that occurred in the county at 7:58 AM Apr 3.
- Officials reported 3 fatalities near Taroko Gorge and another fatality near the Da Qing Shui Tunnel on the Suhua Highway due to falling rocks.

- At least 57 others in the county had been injured.
- The earthquake caused at least 26 buildings to collapse.
- Offices and schools across Hualien County and 6 schools in Taipei had been suspended.
- A total of 354,543 households had lost power following the earthquake.
- Reports indicated some internet outages in parts of Taiwan.
- Numerous roads and highways were closed due to damage and landslides.
- Hualien's Qingshui bridge had completely collapsed.
- Train systems in Taiwan were temporarily suspended to check for damage.
- Sea routes had been added to alleviate traffic along the east coast.

Some more information followed, specifically on Taroko, Hualien.

- TAIPEI (Taiwan News) - In the wake of a 7.4 magnitude earthquake that struck Taiwan's east coast on Wednesday (Apr 3) morning, landslides had cut off access along Hualien's Provincial Highway 8, which led in and out of Taroko National Park.
- An estimated 50 employees of the Silks Place Hotel were travelling to work in 4 shuttle buses and were stranded on the mountainous road as a result of the landslides.
- Based on the time the shuttle buses headed up the mountain and pings picked up from the cell phone service towers, authorities believed the group may have sought shelter in the Jiuqiu cave system (Tunnel of Nine Turns) after the initial quake.
- In an area with normally unstable cell phone service, there were worries that the entrance to the tunnel or the cave may have collapsed or otherwise been sealed by rockfall during the numerous aftershocks.
- By afternoon on Wednesday, 3 April, emergency crews had begun the arduous work of clearing the road to rescue the group.

Normally, earthquakes with deeper epicentres posed a reduced risk of aftershocks. However, our experience with a shallow quake meant that aftershocks would persist, leaving us unable to anticipate their frequency or severity. Officials stated that due to constant aftershocks, it was impossible to carry out emergency repairs until the situation stabilised.

1:00 PM

More updates came in...

- 9 victims, 143 injured (20 hospitalised), 111 sheltered.
- Meanwhile, 75 people stranded in various tunnels in Hualien County had been rescued by emergency responders. As of 7 AM, Thursday, 4 April, 137 people remained trapped.
- Two German citizens who were caught up earlier in a tunnel in Hualien County had been rescued. Rescuers were en route to 12 people, including 2 Canadians, stuck on a trail in Taroko Gorge.
- Most of those trapped were in 2 road tunnels in northern Hualien County. The 400-metre Junwen Tunnel, where 60 people were trapped, is one of more than a dozen tunnels that thread the Suhua highway–a scenic but treacherous and narrow road that runs for 118 kilometres along the east coast.
- Road crews were working to clear rocks and earth as they moved westward and upward into the mountainous terrain of the Taroko National Park. At the 180 km mark of the provincial highway, crews found a jeep on the road with one dead passenger who had been crushed by a falling boulder.
- By 7 PM Wednesday, crews had cleared approximately 8 km from the Jiuqiu cave system entrance. If work continued without major delays, they may reach the area where the employees are thought to be trapped sometime after midnight on Thursday, Apr 4.

- Farther up the mountain, at the Silks Place Resort, 309 guests were reportedly staying at the hotel the morning of the earthquake. All of the hotel guests were reportedly safe despite being temporarily stranded in the Taroko National Park.
- Due to the continued risk of aftershocks and falling rocks over the coming days, the government warned the public to stay out of Taiwan's National Parks and away from the remote mountain roads until further notice.

I read all these updates, but I couldn't really focus. My eyes were seeing the words, but my brain could not comprehend anything. All I could do was continuously ruminate in the disbelief of what we had experienced in the past 30 hours, wondering how much longer we would have to bear the ordeal, and how we would ever get out of there.

Somewhere in the distance, I heard a loud roaring sound of a chopper descending into the hotel parking lot. It came bearing essential supplies including food and water, and to evacuate people with medical emergencies.

The Local Community

1:30 PM (+1 day)

The emergency helicopter's descent into the hotel parking lot stirred a frenzy among the gathered crowd. Cameras clicked frantically to capture its arrival with a sense of urgency bordering on desperation. As the chopper touched down, a gust of wind uprooted plants and trees in its wake.

Some cargo of supplies was dropped, and a handful of people were ushered aboard and whisked away to safety. For the rest of us left behind, resignation mingled with hope as we watched the helicopter take off, leaving behind a longing for escape. Though the allure of escape beckoned, we resigned ourselves to the reality of waiting.

Gearóid and Claire, who had kindly offered us their room, also told us about a business centre on the third floor of the hotel. They mentioned it had a few couches we could use to rest, away from the hustle and bustle in the lobby area. However, they cautioned us about the heightened intensity of aftershocks experienced on higher floors compared to ground level–a vital piece of information that eased our anxieties as the tremors persisted.

We found our way to the business centre. The room boasted 8 long, cushioned benches lining the walls, accompanied by a massive conference-style table surrounded by chairs at its centre. Cosy sit-out areas, complete with coffee tables and chairs, dotted the perimeter, offering secluded spots for rest.

Business Centre at Silks Place Hotel, Taroko, with views of the
mountains and river

We grabbed a cushion each and tried to sleep. But sleep was elusive as the persistent buzzing of my phone interrupted any chance of respite. Finally, I relented and answered an unrecognised number–it was our Airbnb host, Linda.

"Hello Linda, this is Nam. We are alright. We were trapped in the tunnel overnight, but we managed to reach the Silks Place Hotel in Taroko. We are safe here. I apologise that we won't be able to check out as planned today," I explained, my voice carrying a mixture of relief and exhaustion.

"Oh my God, oh my God, I am so happy you are okay. Thank God you are okay. May God bless you. You are so lucky; you are so blessed. Thank goodness, I am so happy to hear your voice!" Linda exclaimed, her words rushing forth in a torrent of relief and gratitude. She had reached out to the authorities, sharing a photo of us captured by her security camera, fearing the worst after the earthquake.

"Gautam sustained a minor injury and requires medical attention, but overall, we are managing. It is uncertain how long our stay here will extend–it might be a few days until we can safely return. How are things on your end?" I inquired, aware of Linda's residence in Hualien.

"Everything is under control here," she reassured, her voice brimming with sincerity. "Please prioritise your well-being and take all the time you require. There is no rush at all–you are welcome to stay in the house for as long as necessary. If you need anything at all, just let me know. And please, do not concern yourself about your car, train, or flight arrangements. I will take care of everything. Thank God you are safe. You are incredibly fortunate, truly blessed."

Oh, Linda! Speaking to her was not very different from the conversation I had with my own family. Her genuine concern and relief could be felt in every word. The warmth in her voice prompted another wave of emotions coursing through me, bringing me to the brink of yet another meltdown. How did we get so lucky?

As I grappled with this overwhelming sense of gratitude, another phone call interrupted my reverie. This time, it was from our parent's network. Through their connections with the India-Taiwan Association, they had identified a contact–a professor residing in Hualien. He had taken on the responsibility of liaising with the car rental company and the embassies to explore options for Gautam's medical evacuation. As they suggested, we prepared to visit a police station to file a report, hopeful that it would expedite the process of securing assistance.

2:45 PM, I wake Gautam from his rest and make our way to the reception, to seek directions to the nearest police station. "I'm sorry, there is no police station in this town," the receptionist informs me. "What do you need?"

"My husband has been injured and requires urgent medical attention. The India-Taiwan Association has requested emergency evacuation from authorities, but they have advised us to file a police report," I explained, my voice tinged with urgency.

"Unfortunately, we don't have a police station in this town." However, the receptionist offered to call a resident doctor to assist with treating the injury and advise on the next steps.

A short while later, a couple of doctors, Dr. Hassan and Aliya, arrived to assist us. They conducted a thorough examination of Gautam's injury, cleansing and dressing the wound with care. It became evident that he would require a few stitches. Despite Gautam experiencing some discomfort, there were no signs of infection so far. The doctors provided us with guidance on monitoring for potential complications—redness, pus, and heightened pain—all indicators of infection. As a precautionary measure, we requested antibiotics from the hotel, but their supply was limited to just 3-4 tablets, likely lasting only a day.

The hotel contacted a representative who sought guidance from the doctors on the appropriate course of action. The diagnosis was sobering. Gautam had sustained 2 deep lacerations on the left side of his face. Without treatment, the risk of infection loomed large, potentially leading to fever and, in the long term, the loss of an earlobe. While the injuries could be addressed with sutures if available onsite, the absence of such supplies necessitated consideration of evacuation.

3:30 PM

With no sutures at hand, a request for an airlift was dispatched to the authorities.

Doctor's examination in the hotel lobby

Large laceration to left earlobe and laceration to left cheek. Both areas requiring sutures. Area cleansed with saline and gauze dressing applied. No current bleeding or signs of infection at this time. Area re-dressed. Discussed signs and symptoms of infection.
Recommend suturing and if any sign of infection, then start p.o. antibiotics.

H. Mighty MD

Diagnosis sent to request medical evacuation

Taroko from Above

3:55 PM (+1 day)

25 minutes later, we found ourselves providing our names and passport details to the authorities, who guided us towards a makeshift helipad in the hotel parking lot. The deafening roar of a chopper heralded its arrival as it descended, and we were prompted with basic questions communicated through signs.

"Are you injured?" the rescuer gestured.

Gautam nodded, indicating the bandaged area on his face and ear.

"Can you walk into the chopper?" the rescuer queried.

Again, Gautam nodded affirmatively.

The same questions were posed to me, and I responded that I was physically unharmed. With instructions to stay low and follow closely, we boarded the helicopter. Inside, there were 4 seats, with an empty space in front, likely reserved for a stretcher. Gautam and I took 2 seats while a rescue marshal occupied the third, leaving one empty. Four other rescuers accompanied us, tasked with piloting the helicopter and scanning the terrain below for survivors.

Hotel parking lot converted into a helipad

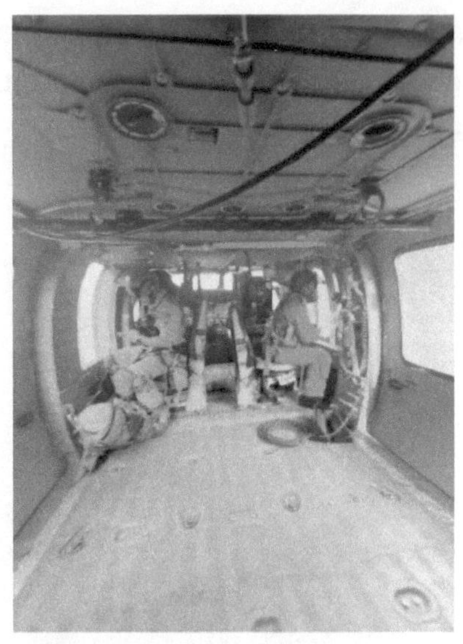

Open windows as rescue marshals looked into the valley below for other people to be evacuated

As we soared away from the hotel, I started to feel it again. An overwhelming sense of

- Relief. Were we really getting out?
- Gratitude. Recognising that Gautam's injury may have facilitated our evacuation.
- Regret. For leaving behind others in the hotel. The fellow hikers and people who had aided us in our time of need.
- Anxiety. This was still not over. It might be safer outside the National Park, but we would still be in Hualien, the epicentre of tectonic activity.

Lost in my thoughts, I occasionally emerged from my reverie to ensure Gautam's well-being while the rescuers maintained a vigilant watch over the mountains and gorge below. From our aerial vantage point, the view was both stunning and surreal—a picturesque National Park veiled in a dust haze, with landslides visible from above, and clouds of smoky dust obscuring the green. Meanwhile, the Liwu River flowed serenely, unperturbed by the turmoil around it, dutifully carving its path through the mountains and deepening the gorge with each passing day.

View of the mountains, landslides still occurring as aftershocks continued

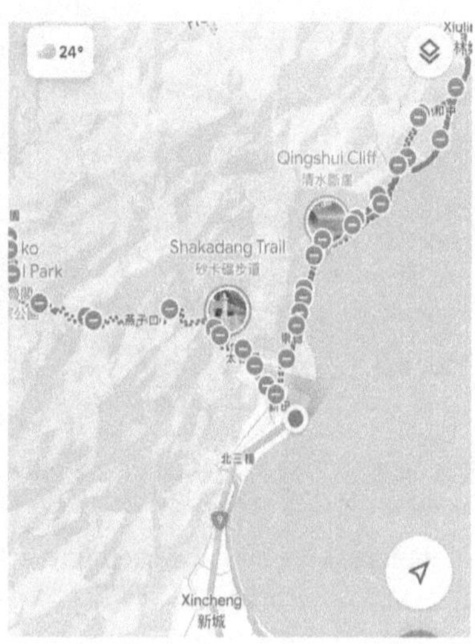

Roads to Taroko National Park closed

4:25 PM When we touched down in an open field in Hualien, we were greeted by a swarm of news and media vans. As we disembarked from the chopper, we were escorted into an ambulance. With my phone battery dwindling, I found myself inundated with calls and messages, now that cell reception was somewhat stable outside the National Park. Assuming the responsibility of keeping our worried families informed of our whereabouts and progress, I relayed updates about the whirlwind of activity. The suddenness of our airlift left everyone, including ourselves, surprised at the rapid turn of events.

The ambulance transported us to a designated site established to offer basic medical assistance to all rescued individuals. As we journeyed, nearing the entrance of Taroko National Park, the sight of the looming mountains in the distance sparked unease within me.

Were we being led back towards the mountains? I hesitated, voicing my concerns, "Where are we headed?"

"Just a little further, almost there, 2 more minutes," came the response.

4:50 PM The medical camp hums with activity, a temporary structure hastily erected to address the urgent needs of evacuees. Inside, a single row of tables is manned by a number of medics, while 2 rows of stools accommodate those awaiting attention. As we enter, Gautam takes the lead, fielding inquiries about his injury from the attending medic– where it hurts, whether he can move his jaw, any other head or eye injuries etc. I follow suit, answering the same questions as a healthcare worker checks my blood pressure and pulse.

I join Gautam, when a BBC news reporter approaches, introducing himself and posing a simple question, "What is it like over there?"

Emotion overwhelms me and tears well up once more. "It is unimaginable," I choke out, my voice shaking. "Like scenes from an apocalyptic movie. It has been a harrowing ordeal..." As I speak, several other news channels converge, their microphones thrust towards me, camera shutters clicking in a frenzy.

5:15 PM We are ushered back into an ambulance. This time, we are bound for the Hualien Hospital. The makeshift rescue camp lacks the facilities to suture wounds, necessitating a trip to the emergency room.

A trapped tourist of Taroko National Park walks to an ambulance after being rescued in Hualien County, eastern Taiwan, Thursday.(AP)

Media frenzy as we landed

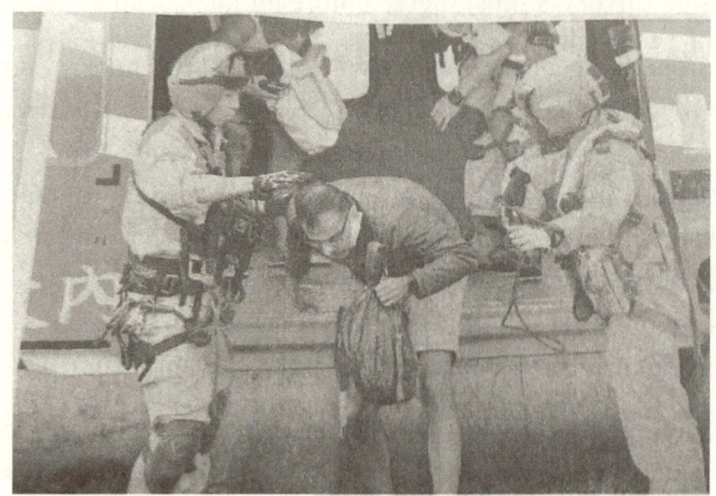

News coverage of initial evacuees

Medics tending to people evacuated from the National Park

Comfort in Strangers

5:30 PM (+1 day)

In the bustling emergency room, we found ourselves in the company of another family of earthquake survivors–they were a family of American and Taiwanese heritage. Comprising 2 young daughters along with their parents, the family was from North Carolina and had been visiting Taiwan for a holiday. Their tranquil morning drive turned into a nightmare when the earthquake struck, sending rocks cascading through the open sunroof. One of the girls suffered a laceration to the back of her head after a stone penetrated the sunroof of their car. Presently, she was getting stitches in the operating room.

The remaining family members bore numerous cuts and scratches from the onslaught of sharp debris as they sought refuge in a nearby tunnel. Abandoning their vehicle, they sprinted to safety, spending the night holed up until rescue teams reached them during the evacuation efforts in the park.

For 2 days, they had lacked access to the amenities that we had seen– showers, clean clothes, food, or water. They appeared muddy and weary from the ordeal. Yet, somehow, the family maintained an admirable sense of resilience. Laughter and light-hearted banter filled the air, a testament to their bond.

When we arrived at the hospital, the language barrier once again presented a challenge, as the admission staff spoke little English. Thankfully, the compassionate man and his elder daughter came to our aid. They facilitated communication, guiding us through the process, translating instructions from the doctor in real-time as he tended to Gautam's injuries and administered a tetanus shot.

5:40 PM Entering the operating room, Gautam received 2 injections of local anaesthesia directly into the lacerations, followed by the sutures. Though he endured physical discomfort, I shared in his pain–a curious phenomenon brought about by love. All I could do was hold his hand tightly, offering silent reassurances that it would soon be over.

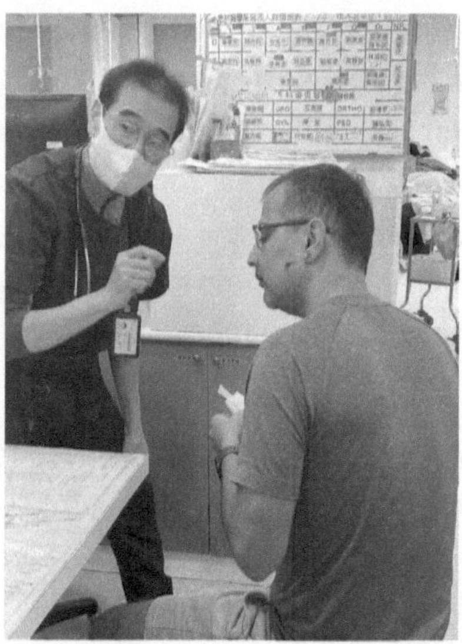

Doctor explains the treatment plan

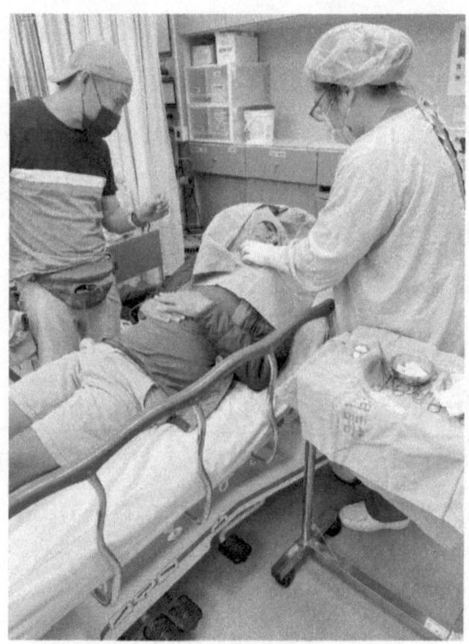

Travel planning for our next trip to Taiwan–the perfect distraction for Gautam

Then, the father of the girls came to Gautam's aid. Engaging him in light conversation, he skilfully diverted Gautam's attention from the discomfort of the sutures piercing his skin. He spoke of other picturesque parts of Taiwan, planting seeds for future visits. I couldn't help but wonder how he knew exactly what would distract Gautam at that moment.

After collecting the prescribed medications and noting instructions for wound care, we settled the bills and bid farewell to the family, wishing them luck and fewer adventures during their remaining time in Taiwan. While waiting for a taxi to take us back to our Airbnb, I glanced up at the sky for the first time in what felt like ages. As I held Gautam's hand, a wave of relief washed over me. It seemed that the worst was finally behind us, and we were safe at last.

"It's okay, we are alright," I whispered, reassuring both him and myself. "It is going to be okay. We got incredibly lucky."

An Angel in Disguise

7:00 PM (+1 day)

Our Airbnb host proved to be a guardian angel, arranging a taxi to whisk us from the hospital back to the comforting familiarity of our temporary home in Hualien. Her actions of care were like a warm embrace after the ordeal, from replenishing our supplies to organising a comforting dinner and leaving behind a thoughtful present. With her presence in town, it was as though we had family in Hualien, her caring voice echoing relief and gratitude that we had returned safely.

Though the earthquake was not her doing, she expressed sincere apologies for what we had been through. Her earnest desire to alleviate our pain, ensure our safety, and make us feel at ease reflected her genuine kindness. The touching gift–a mountain marble souvenir bearing a timeless quote: 'May you always find peace when you see the mountains', was such a kind and thoughtful reminder for us not to be afraid despite life's uncertainties.

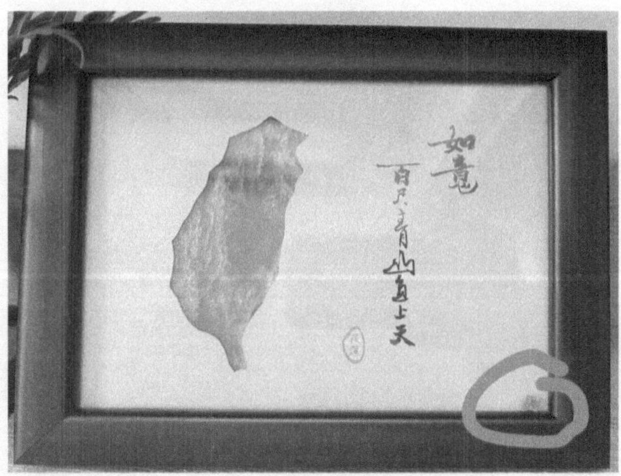

Mountain marble souvenir. A gift from our Airbnb host.
Encircled is a piece of stone from the mountain that fell into my clothes during the earthquake. I brought it back as a souvenir.

9:00 PM We settled back into our Airbnb and regained access to chargers. Our first priority was reconnecting with family and reassuring friends who had been anxiously checking in. Deciding to extend our stay for another day or 2 seemed like the best course of action, allowing us the time to recuperate from the trauma we had endured.

The prospect of a peaceful night's sleep and the comfort of a familiar kitchen, where I could prepare nourishing meals while tending to Gautam's wounds, held immense appeal. However, our hopes for rest were swiftly dashed by the relentless activity of the tectonic plates, which showed no signs of abating after 36 hours of continuous movement.

With each new aftershock, some registering at magnitudes of 5 or higher, the very foundations of our Airbnb seemed to quake. The walls and ceilings reverberated with a rattling sound, and the giant scarlet macaw in my body re-emerged, ready to fight or flight each time. The instinct to flee, to seek refuge beneath the open sky where the threat of landslides was less imminent, surged to the forefront of my mind with each tremor.

But the town remained calm and sleepy through the night. The tremors persisted, each rumble accompanied by the ominous clatter and vibrations, prompting Gautam and me to exchange anxious glances.

"Is it happening again, or am I imagining this?" I whispered.

"No, it's happening. I feel it too," Gautam confirmed, his expression mirroring my uncertainty.

"Should we evacuate?" I questioned, my nerves on edge.

"I am so exhausted. Can we just sit for a little while longer?" Gautam replied wearily.

But before we could even consider our options, the tremors intensified, and the cacophony of noises grew louder and more ominous.

Grrrrr, clang, clang, thud.

At that moment, instinct overrode exhaustion. Panic surged, urging us to flee.

"RUN. GET OUT. GET OUT. NOW," I exclaimed, urgency colouring my words as we scrambled to seek safety outside.

On the streets, the only sounds were those of cicadas chirping, frogs croaking, and other nocturnal creatures stirring in the darkness. Our neighbours slept peacefully, undisturbed by the tremors that had become our unwelcome companions. For us, with each attempt to get some rest, the bed trembled, jolting us awake.

10:30 PM Faced with the impracticality of fleeing outside each time, we devised a strategy: to seek refuge beneath the bed at the next sign of tremors. In our small home, devoid of any towering structures, hiding under the bed seemed like the most viable option to shield ourselves from potential harm. Despite the looming danger of a collapsed roof, we found a strange sense of reassurance in the knowledge that, somehow, we would survive the weight of a wooden beam fallen on our heads.

Indeed, through the turmoil, there were glimpses of resilience. The trauma we endured provided us with a newfound perspective... Until the next major aftershock reactivated the same neural pathways that kept us safe through the ordeal, refusing to grant us the peace we so desperately sought.

Farewell, Hualien

2:00 AM (+2 days)

Awake in the middle of the night, our bodies weary from the relentless tremors, we knew we could not endure much longer. The idea of home beckoned, promising the solace of familiar surroundings and much-needed rest. Though our original plans had us lingering in Taiwan for another week, exploring Kenting, a picturesque beach town on the southern coast, and the tranquil Sun Moon Lake before returning for our flight out of Taipei, the experience had shifted our priorities entirely.

The car rental company, empathetic to our plight, had offered a replacement vehicle for the remainder of our stay. However, neither of us felt fit to take the wheel. Instead, I called Singapore Airlines to reschedule our flight while Gautam made train reservations to ferry us from Hualien back to Taipei. With our bags packed, we informed our Airbnb host of our plans to leave at 9 AM.

8:30 AM True to her caring nature, Linda arrived early, bearing breakfast–Taiwanese black tea, and a warm smile to welcome us back. Her concern for our well-being was palpable, as she recounted her anxious attempts to reach us in the aftermath of the earthquake. With heartfelt blessings and a prayer for our safety, she extended an invitation for us to return to her home anytime we wished, emphasising that this town would always be our home.

At the train station, Linda's friend, the owner of a souvenir shop, joined us to offer traditional good luck charms. These vibrant tokens of goodwill, tied snugly around our wrists, lifted our spirits and brought back a smile from our faces all the way to our hearts. The charm, like a friendship band, was a symbol of the kindness and generosity of strangers in our time of need. Their whispered chants echoed in my heart, promising safe passage on our journey home.

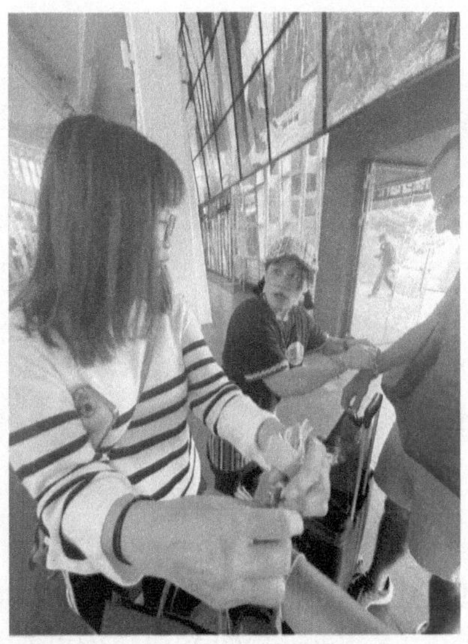

Departing from Xincheng with blessings and good luck charms

Final goodbye to Taroko, with gratitude for everything we experienced

10:40 AM The newly constructed train station, boasting a breathtaking vista of the majestic Taroko National Park mountains, appeared strangely foreboding on that day. Heavy clouds loomed overhead; their dark presence cast a sombre filter over the landscape. In the aftermath of the earthquake, rainfall was expected–a natural consequence of landslides that accompanied the seismic activity. As I looked at the ominous sky, my thoughts turned to our fellow hikers who remained trapped in the confines of the Silks Place Hotel, nestled among the towering peaks of the mountains.

'I hope they're okay,' I mused silently, 'I hope the rain and weather conditions do not impede the rescue teams from reaching them safely.'

11:30 AM The train arrived, and we settled into our seats. Linda had thoughtfully packed us a hearty lunch and a delectable local dessert.

Soon after the train departed for Taipei, we delved into our provisions, savouring the picturesque landscapes that unfolded outside our windows. Lush fields, quaint towns, rugged coastal cliffs, and turquoise waters passed by as people revelled in outdoor activities. I watched hikers on the trails and wondered when I would feel ready to embark on my next hiking adventure. Would I ever hike again? I hoped so.

The train continued its journey towards Taipei, weaving through tunnels and countryside landscapes. Still, I could not shake the sensation of ongoing aftershocks. Despite the rhythmic motion of the train and the unsettling movement of the tectonic plates below, I hoped that the railway tracks would endure and safely transport us to our destination. It would be some time before I could believe that the ordeal was truly over.

Too Soon, Taiwan

1:30 PM (+2 days)

When the train pulled into Taipei's main station, the bustling energy of the city greeted us like an old friend. It was as if the earthquake, just 2 days prior, had been but a fleeting interruption to the rhythm of daily life. Despite lingering aftershocks, the people of Taipei carried on, accustomed to the occasional tremor. Boarding the train bound for Taoyuan International Airport, we found ourselves amidst the ebb and flow of commuters, the familiar sights and sounds offering a sense of normalcy amid the chaos.

Barely a week ago, we had eagerly stepped through the gates of this very airport, bubbling with excitement for our holiday. However, our plans were overshadowed by the ordeal we endured. Seven days felt like an eternity, as we navigated through uncertainty and fear over the past 2 days. Yet the kindness of the Taiwanese people left an indelible mark on our hearts, instilling within us a desire to return someday and complete the rest of our unfinished itinerary.

Photo promoting views of the Tunnel with Nine Turns at Taoyuan International Airport, Taipei

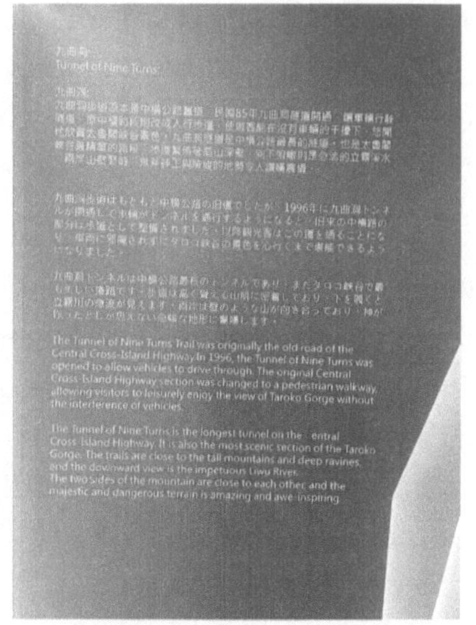

Life-size poster of The Tunnel of Nine Turns at the airport

5:00 PM We walked through the terminal towards our boarding gate when a poster caught my eye, depicting the Tunnel of Nine Turns. It read:

"The Tunnel of Nine Turns was originally the old road of the Central Cross-Island Highway. In 1996, the Tunnel of Nine Turns was opened to allow vehicles to drive through. The original Central Cross-Island Highway section was changed to a pedestrian walkway, allowing visitors to leisurely enjoy the view of Taroko Gorge without the interference of vehicles.

The Tunnel of Nine Turns is the longest tunnel on the Central Cross-Island Highway. It is also the most scenic section of the Taroko Gorge. The trails are close to the tall mountains and deep ravines, and the downward view is the impetuous Liwu River. The 2 sides of the mountain are close to each other, and the majestic and dangerous terrain is amazing and awe-inspiring."

The image evoked a visceral response within me, triggering a rush of anxiety and a longing to be by Gautam's side. Here in the airport's bustling activity, the dissonance between the world outside and what I felt within was palpable. But we were on the other side now, and I just felt so grateful to be there.

We settled into our seats on the flight, trying to find some semblance of normalcy despite the lingering chaos of the past days. The captain's announcements were lost on me; my brain felt scrambled, and my body still stupefied. But the familiar melody of Singapore Airlines music and safety video brought a comforting sense of routine. As the plane took off, the turbulence was a rude reminder of the aftershocks.

Unable to find rest, my thoughts spiralled in a ceaseless loop of disbelief, gratitude, and shock. Each emotion crashed into the next, leaving me feeling unsettled and disoriented. Hours passed in a blur until, finally, the plane touched down in Singapore.

Outside the arrival lounge at Changi Airport, a reporter awaited us, recognising Gautam from the news coverage in Taiwan. He approached us, eager to hear our story for an article. Though weary from our journey, I wanted to share the experience, believing it could offer perspective and reach others. I provided him with my contact information, promising to speak with him the next day, after we had rested.

10:30 PM Finally home, I reflected on the countless moments over the past 56 hours when the prospect of returning seemed bleak. Yet, against all odds, we made it back, filled with a newfound appreciation for life and all its blessings. Grateful for our safety and the opportunity to reunite with loved ones, I couldn't help but smile at the sound of my husband's deep, throaty snores - a reminder of the precious moments we still have to spend together.

Coverage in various news articles

It was a nightmare, got stuck in tunnel for 24 hrs: Indian woman on Taiwan earthquake

Indian woman Namrata Kohli said she and her husband "spent 24 hours holed up in a tunnel" amid the recent Taiwan earthquake that hit while they were hiking in Taroko National Park. "Gautam (husband)...got stitches on his face and ear from being hit by a rock that came like a meteor," said Kohli. "It was a nightmare," she added.

short by Sakshita Khosla / 07 Apr, 2024

Digital news reports

The Others in Taroko

3 days after the Earthquake

Even upon our return home, my thoughts lingered in Taroko. I could not stop thinking about those trapped alongside us in the tunnel–those who trekked to the Silks Place Hotel, those left behind, and the generous hotel guests who offered their resources to ease our discomfort and ensure our safety. My days were consumed by updates from Taiwan news, and I was desperate to connect with those affected.

The TV delivered news of a relentless stream of aftershocks and rain, hindering rescue efforts. Each report of a rising death toll–from 7 to 11, then 13–felt like a tightening knot in my chest. Physically unscathed, yet emotionally raw, I couldn't shake the feeling that it could easily have been us, another statistic on the news. Among the missing were a Singaporean couple last seen on the Shakadang Trail[6]; I hoped that they would soon be found.

I kept in touch with friends at the Silks Place Hotel. Thankfully, they remained safe, but as a nearby hotel lost power overnight, more evacuees sought refuge at the Silks Place Hotel. Despite being a fully functional five-star hotel, resources and supplies had to be rationed. Full-service meals were scaled back to basics–carbs, vegetables, and a protein. Fortunately, network services gradually resumed, allowing individuals to reconnect with loved ones.

However, it took them another 2 nights to escape Taroko. With the eastward road still closed, those not airlifted out had to drive in the opposite direction, reaching Taichung on the west coast before doubling back to Hualien on the east. There, they collected their belongings and travel documents before heading to Taipei.

Two days later, we caught sight of the Tunnel with Nine Turns survivors on the news.[7]

"That's Alice!!" I exclaimed as I saw her face on TV.

"They found Li! Thank goodness they made it to the tunnel," I said with relief.

Accompanied by rescue personnel, they looked battered but resilient. Despite their injuries, they would receive the necessary medical care and pull through.

1 week after the Earthquake

Alena returned to Singapore, and we reunited the following week. It was a heartwarming moment to reconnect with her in the safety and comfort of a familiar environment at home. We exchanged stories of the experience and swapped photos and contacts of those who journeyed with us through the tunnel and the hotel.

I have remained in contact with many of the people we met in Taroko National Park. Our bond was forged through the shared ordeal of surviving a period of life-threatening adversity together. They have checked in on Gautam's recovery, and we have continued to exchange stories of our travels and photos since our return home. Remarkably, we have received invitations to visit their home and family in Taiwan, and various other parts of the world.

I am certain that each person grappled with their own worries and anxieties during that time, just as I did. Physically, we were fortunate to emerge relatively unscathed, given the circumstances. However, the mental toll of such an experience will be a journey for us all. While some may have faced greater challenges in the past, for me, who has enjoyed a mostly sheltered and comfortable life, this event has had a profound impact on both my mind and body. I will delve deeper into these aspects in the upcoming chapters.

PART 6

Reflections and Resilience

Ripples of the Quake

In the aftermath of the earthquake, I discovered that the trauma extended far beyond the epicentre. It wasn't just us or the other visitors in Taroko National Park who suffered; our families, friends, and loved ones endured their own versions of the ordeal. The initial shock came when they heard about the earthquake on the news and saw the devastating footage. The panic intensified when they tried to reach us, only to be met with silence.

As hours passed without any contact, imaginations ran wild, conjuring worst-case scenarios. Desperation drove them to take action, leading to the formation of makeshift search and rescue taskforces composed of our parents, siblings, and closest friends. Within hours of the news breaking, my brother and a few friends tracked us down on Instagram. They pieced together our last known location from my stories, deducing that we were likely in or around the Tunnel of Nine Turns.

Though this discovery provided a clue, it offered no confirmation of our well-being. Each member of our circle grappled with the same haunting fear–that we were either fatally injured or buried alive. Yet, they maintained a facade of strength and calm to avoid spreading panic, each person silently battling their own uncertainty and dread.

Frantic calls were made, and networks were activated as everyone tried to reach out to anyone they knew in Taiwan. They sought help in translating, connecting with authorities, and gathering any available information about our whereabouts and condition. Copies of our photographs, passports, and the last videos I posted were circulated widely. Our names were posted on various sites and forums in a desperate bid for news.

The complexity of our names in Chinese led to multiple variations, resulting in a search not just for 2 Indian nationals, but for 4 additional fictitious people with names similar to ours. This confusion became apparent when authorities began asking if we knew someone named 'Anam Pata,' along with a phone number that turned out to be a garbled version of my own.

When Uri and 3 others from the tunnel reached the Silks Place Hotel in Taroko on the evening of the quake, they had the list of contact details with them. As promised, they made calls to inform our families of our well-being in the Tunnel of Nine Turns. My parents, already grief-stricken and panic-struck, answered a call from an unfamiliar Taiwan number. When they were informed of our safety, relief washed over them, but so did a wave of scepticism. They needed to hear our voices to believe it was true, fearing it might be a cruel hoax.

Until we emerged from the tunnel and spoke with them directly, our friends and families endured a relentless ordeal of anxiety and fear. Their struggle was different from ours, but no less severe. They longed for our safe return, to see us, hear our voices, hug us, and confirm with their own senses that we were indeed alive and well.

Reading about two missing Indian people[8] in the aftermath of a catastrophic earthquake would undoubtedly strike fear into any family's heart. Our loved ones suffered immensely, their anguish amplified by the distance and the lack of concrete information. Once we made contact and were reunited, a new phase of recovery began, not just for us but for everyone who had been caught in the ripple effect of that terrifying day.

Life After Trauma

A month on...

I do not feel like the same person who walked into the Tunnel of Nine Turns the morning of 3-Apr 2024. I am a changed person–the things I value, what I want from life, the things I react to, and how I feel. There are multiple changes I have noticed–some physical, others emotional. Some are good and others unwelcome, but I am on a journey to explore each one of them and understand how they serve me.

Diagnosed with 'acute stress reaction,' I feel aftershocks almost everywhere I go -

- On a turbulent flight.
- When the next-door apartment undergoing renovation starts drilling.
- When I cross a busy street.
- When a plane flies close overhead.
- When a loud *thud* sounds in the distance.
- Sometimes, when Gautam shakes his leg on the bed.

I feel a physical reaction to perceived danger -

- I feel danger far more easily.
- Vigilance in my nervous system is persistently on, and it is exhausting.
- A fire turns on in my legs, making me ready to fight or take flight at a moment's notice.
- It is that same giant scarlet macaw trapped inside my belly, flapping its wings wildly, creating jitters in my gut and generating spasms in every inch of my quads and calves.
- My stomach hurts almost every evening since the experience.

- I experience unexplained spikes in my heart rate when I feel threatened, including dogs and cats (and I love dogs... or at least I used to).

Emotionally, I get overwhelmed far more easily

- I cannot watch the news without feeling guilty about the trauma people are experiencing.
- I cry when I watch movies, or any content based on a theme of separation.
- But I am okay. I just need to rest it off and reset.

On the positive,

- I feel gratitude for every little thing we have.
- I feel so much more present in my relationships than I ever did.
- I have a newfound appreciation for nature and find myself paying attention.
- I am less easily distracted by screens and social media, which naturally allows me to be more intentional.
- I am enamoured by the idea of escaping big-city life and the stimuli presented by capitalism.
- I am reminded every day of how little I need to be truly happy.
- I recognise my emotions and give myself the space to feel what I am feeling rather than trying to 'keep it together.'
- Another fascinating positive is how many of my pains have suddenly reduced–almost disappeared. I used to complain of a tennis elbow and 2 busted ligaments on my right ankle, impacting my stability. Since the experience, my ankle pain has disappeared, and my elbow has improved faster than it did after several physiotherapy sessions. Initially, I thought it was the adrenaline powering my body, taking all pains away. But a month on, I have figured it is an 'increased pain threshold' which usually accompanies combat-related PTSD. How cool is that?

Finding Strength in Moving On

We have talked to friends and family, baring our souls and sharing the excruciating details of the experience. Photographs accompanied our words, serving as visual aids to explain the where, how, what, and why of it all. It was a cathartic process, a release of pent-up emotions that had been weighing heavy on our hearts.

Once the intimate conversations with loved ones were over, I took to social media[9] and spoke with the real media.[10] I felt compelled to share our story with a wider audience, to shine a light on the darkness we had endured. There was a sense of urgency, a need to ensure that our voices were heard.

Every morning, I wake up with a spring in my step, excited to write about it all. There is something inside me that believes this experience is worthy of an audience, that perhaps someday, someone will decide to turn it into a documentary or a movie. It is a strange feeling to find purpose in pain, but it is one that drives me forward.

Each time I sit down to write about the experience, it brings back memories, both painful and poignant. But in revisiting those moments, I find closure, a way to process the ordeal and make sense of it all.

In a strange way, writing about it feels like I am filing it away, neatly packaging it up and tucking it into the recesses of my mind. My aim is to publish a blog and share our story with the world, and then, perhaps, it will be out of my system.

But then I wonder, do I even want to get it out of my system? Maybe not. Maybe I am better for having had this experience, scars and all. I am seeking professional help to process it, to unpack the emotions and make peace with the past.

Every day, I see Gautam; his scar is a visible reminder of what we went through together. And in that reminder, I find strength. It serves as a daily prompt to be grateful, to be more present, and to live each day with intention.

I smile, I laugh, and I talk to friends and family. I watch movies and binge Netflix. But in the midst of the laughter and the chatter, there is a quieter yet more tumultuous undercurrent to my life.

I am triggered by loud sounds. An incoming train rumbling through the station sets my heart racing. Turbulence on a flight sends shivers down my spine. Even the renovation in the unit next-door feels like an assault on my senses. In the dead of night, I wake up with my mind racing. Cold sweats drench my sheets, and my muscles ache from the tension. It is as if my body refuses to grant me the peace I seek.

Crossing the road, I sometimes freeze like a deer caught in headlights. My body rebels, refusing to move forward, paralysed by uncertainty. And then there are the tears. They come at unexpected times, catching me off guard. Whether it is while wishing someone a happy birthday, brushing my teeth, or simply witnessing a tender moment between loved ones, the tears flow freely. And I have come to realise that it is okay to cry.

But amidst the chaos of my emotions, I am finding solace in seeking help. Therapy has become my anchor, providing me with the tools and support I need to navigate this turbulent sea of emotions. Writing has become my creative outlet, a way to make sense of the jumble of thoughts swirling around in my mind. Through pen and paper, I am able to give voice to the turmoil within me, finding clarity and understanding in the process.

I am learning to find my balance, to give myself the time and grace to heal. It is a journey fraught with ups and downs, but I owe it to myself and to the people I love to keep moving forward, one step at a time. I am grateful to be here, to have the opportunity to tell my story. And I hope that by sharing my struggles, I can offer a glimmer of hope to others who may be facing similar challenges.

If you are struggling, know that you are not alone. It is okay to ask for help and lean on others for support. Your journey may be different from mine, but I believe that with courage and resilience, you will find your way out of the darkness and into the light.

Navigating Differences and Embracing Joy

Every Day Since the Earthquake...

We all process things differently. That is a truth I have come to accept, especially in the wake of recent events. While Gautam seems to effortlessly glide through life, I find myself still grappling with the aftershocks of our shared experience. And that's okay. We are each on our own journey, and it is essential to give ourselves and others the space to navigate it in a way that brings us happiness and healing.

Respecting Individual Needs:

Gautam's chill demeanour has been a source of both admiration and bemusement for me. While he finds solace in watching football matches and immersing himself in work, I seek comfort in quieter pursuits like writing to process my feelings. At the end of a long day, he might prefer scrolling through his phone while I yearn for moments of reflection and gratitude. And in the morning, while he is eager to hit the gym, I find solace in putting pen to paper. Our differences are not a source of conflict but rather an opportunity to give each other the space we need to thrive.

Finding Joy in the Everyday:

Despite the chaos and challenges of life, it is essential to find joy in the little things. Sure, birthdays, anniversaries and promotions warrant celebration, but there is equal merit in revelling in the everyday moments of happiness. For Gautam and me, it is the simple pleasures that bring us the most joy–sharing a morning workout, watching TV together, planning budget-friendly holidays, and sharing laughs over home-cooked meals. We have learned that true happiness isn't found in fancy dinners or designer clothes, but in the moments we spend together, cherishing each other's company and the small joys of life.

Prioritising Connection Over Materialism:

Our lifestyle mirrors our values—opting for practicality, we continue to use public transportation, meticulously check price tags, and search for value deals. Flying economy is not about sacrificing comfort but rather about prioritising closeness and connection. We would rather share cramped quarters, holding hands, than indulge in first-class amenities. Our bond is nurtured by everyday gestures of love and companionship, not by extravagant displays.

In the end, it is about honouring our differences, finding joy in the every day, and prioritising connection over materialism. We may process things differently, but in embracing our individual needs and celebrating the little moments, we have found a path to happiness and fulfilment together.

Worst Day of My Life or Best Day?

As I reflect on the events that unfolded, I find myself grappling with a fundamental question: Was it the worst day of my life or the best day?

In the chapters preceding this one, I delved into the depths of despair, recounting the experience of being caught in the worst earthquake Taiwan has seen in a quarter of a century, following which we were trapped in a tunnel for 24 agonising hours. We were in a foreign land with a group of strangers, many of whom did not speak the same language as us.

With each passing moment, we faced the threats of dwindling supplies, mounting uncertainty, and the constant spectre of danger as we confronted our deepest fears about the possibility of never seeing our families again. It was a day marked by fear, desperation, and the realisation of our mortality.

Yet, as I sit here writing this now, I cannot help but wonder if there is more to the story. Could it be that amidst the darkness, there exists a flicker of light? Could the worst day of our lives hold within it the seeds of transformation, resilience, and newfound purpose?

In the midst of our ordeal, it was easy to succumb to despair, to see only the looming shadow of tragedy cast over us. But as time passed and we emerged from the darkness, battered but unbowed, I began to see things differently.

Yes, the day we spent trapped in that tunnel was undoubtedly one of the most challenging experiences of our lives. It tested us in ways we could never have imagined, pushing us to the brink of our physical, emotional, and spiritual limits. But in that suffering, I discovered something profound–a resilience, a strength, a sense of purpose that I never knew I possessed.

It is true that the risk of loss—of money, of loved ones, of life itself—loomed large over us that day. But what if, instead of viewing these risks as sources of despair, we saw them as opportunities for growth and doing things better? What if the very things that threatened to destroy us also held the key to our salvation?

In hindsight, it is plain to see that our darkest moments force us to confront our deepest fears, re-evaluate our priorities, and find strength in times of hardship. And while we may never fully grasp the true significance of those experiences at the moment, we can take solace in the knowledge that they have the potential to shape us in unexpected ways.

So, was it the worst day of my life or the best day? Perhaps it is neither and both. Perhaps it is simply a chapter in the ongoing saga of our lives—a chapter filled with pain, yes, but also with hope, resilience, and the belief that even in our darkest moments, there is a glimmer of light.

Lessons in Resilience

If there is one takeaway I want to leave with anyone reading this book, it is this: Hardships in life are inevitable. If you haven't already faced adversity, you have been lucky. But that lucky streak likely won't last forever. Life has a way of presenting challenges, whether losing a loved one or facing a critical illness. Or if you are like us, you could find yourself caught in a natural disaster while you are on vacation.

On a bright sunny day, without a care in the world, you could get caught in a tsunami, flash flood or a bout of clear air turbulence on a flight. The number of such disasters is increasing and has become a recurring phenomenon when you turn on the news these days. No one is immune forever. While you won't be able to predict or pre-empt these, you can prepare yourself to build resilience to survive the trauma.

Through our experience, I have realised that some of the most fulfilling outcomes in life come to us when we accept adversity for everything it has to offer. Even the worst experiences are worth living through, because they teach us something important about ourselves. Here are some life-lessons I gathered from our experience–these are simple yet powerful things you can incorporate into your daily life to build resilience and live a life without regret.

Build Physical and Mental Strength

Take care of your body. Eat well, exercise regularly, and rest sufficiently. Many of us already practise some form of a healthy lifestyle, and if you haven't started yet, it is never too late. While we were in that tunnel, my practice with intermittent fasting kept me calm on a limited diet, and when we were on that impossible mound, I had multiple flashbacks of moments spent with my fitspo friends, 'fitfluencers,' yoga buddies and every gym trainer, doctor and physiotherapist who helped me build strength and heal my body.

Equally important, is mental health. Build resilience through mindfulness practices. The mind can be a minefield of thoughts. Learn to quiet that noise and tap into a deeper sense of clarity.

Meditation, in particular, can be a powerful tool for cultivating mental strength and resilience. In moments of hardship, it is often our mental fortitude that carries us through, making the mind an asset in navigating life's challenges.

Express Your Love

Tell your loved ones what they mean to you. Do not take your family or friends for granted. Life is a gift, and with each passing year, we are granted the privilege of growing older. Rather than lamenting the passage of time, celebrate it as a testament to the experiences and wisdom gained along the way.

When I was in that tunnel with no contact with the outside world, the one thing that gnawed at me was whether I had ended my last conversation with my family on a positive note. All I wanted was to tell them I loved them, and apologise for any hurt I may have caused. Today, I make it a point to be more intentional and present in my conversations with my family. Every day is an opportunity to seize your relationships with renewed vigour and gratitude.

Trust Your Judgement

During times of adversity, you will feel a loss of control. You will wonder why it's happening to you. You will question what you did to deserve it and you will feel unworthy. You will blame everyone and everything around you. In those moments, focus on what you can control. Recognise that you have a unique skill-set—one that is special and exclusive to you—and it can positively impact both you and those around you. While you might not see it at the moment, time will reveal its significance. So, don't second-guess yourself. You know what you need to do—trust your judgement.

Regret serves little purpose. Understand that every decision is made with the best of intentions and the information available at that time. Instead of dwelling on the past, focus on learning from experiences and moving forward with resilience. On that impossible mound, there were a few moments of fatal distraction when I glanced at the landslide-prone mountain and into the gaping gorge below. But all I needed to do was to trust my ability, put one foot ahead of the other, and keep trudging along.

Embrace Kindness

When faced with adversity, you will encounter acts of kindness all around you. They will come in different forms, and you will be able to tap into your own generosity in fascinating and unexpected ways. Pay attention to your own kindness and notice the kindness around you. Welcome it into your life. In our experience surviving the earthquake, several people brought us first aid, a hotel opened its doors to us, a kind couple offered us clean clothes, an Airbnb host became our family away from home, and an unknown family offered help with translation for us to receive treatment in a hospital.

You will find all the help you need. You just need to find the grace to accept it and then pay it forward.

Process and Heal

Even after the ordeal is over, it may not feel like it is truly over. There is a chance you will bounce back to your old self seamlessly as if nothing ever happened, and that is perfectly fine. But it is equally likely that you will feel like a different person altogether. Not everyone will understand this new mindset, so allow yourself the time to process it in your own way. Each of us is unique, and we cope differently. Some may advise you to forget and move on, which is great if you can, but if you can't, do not bottle it up.

Make no mistake–this newfound perspective is a gift and an opportunity. Pay attention to your emotions and harness the energy they bring. There is strength in vulnerability, and seeking help when needed is a sign of courage, not weakness. Whether it is professional counselling, support groups, or simply reaching out to friends and family, don't hesitate to lean on others for guidance and support.

Live with Purpose and Intent

Life is too short to be spent doing things that don't bring you joy. You cannot even be sure that you will live to see another day, much less several more decades. Whether it is pursuing a career, engaging in hobbies, or spending time with loved ones, find joy in the activities that resonate with your passions. When you align your actions with your true desires, everything becomes more meaningful and fulfilling.

Take the time to explore what truly drives you. Understanding what truly motivates you is essential for living with purpose and intent. For some, it may be the pursuit of personal growth or the desire to make a positive impact on the world. In times of crisis, our priorities become starkly clear, revealing our deepest desires and motivations. Look out for them and adopt these revelations as guiding lights on your journey.

Ultimately, it took a close encounter with my own mortality for me to realise my calling–the desire to survive so that I could share my story with others. In the middle of the crisis, I discovered a newfound sense of purpose. May my journey serve as a reminder to embrace life and cherish each moment as a precious gift.

Our experience in Taroko National Park was a reminder of the fragility of life and the strength of the human spirit. We emerged from that tunnel changed, with a deeper appreciation for life and the people around us. My hope is that you never find yourself in such a dire situation, but if you do, remember to trust your instinct and accept the changes that follow.

Life is unpredictable, but with love, resilience, and gratitude, we can face whatever comes our way.

Gratitude for What Got Us Here

When I reflect on the harrowing journey that brought us to this moment, I am struck by the undeniable truth that it was the convergence of several factors that ultimately led to our survival.

For me, the driving force was a deep-seated determination to live, not just for the sake of existing, but to bear witness and share the story of our resilience and triumph over trauma. The thought of being able to tell our tale to inspire others with our courage and perseverance gave me the strength to keep fighting in the darkest of moments.

For Gautam, it was the simple yet profound realisation that life, despite its challenges and uncertainties, is inherently worth living. With each passing day, he finds meaning in the small joys and blessings that surround us—our happy life, untainted by physical, financial, or mental troubles. It was this enduring belief in the inherent goodness of life that sustained him through the trials of the experience.

But perhaps above all, it was love that proved to be our greatest ally in the battle for survival. In the depths of despair, we found strength in each other's arms, clinging to the bond that held us together through thick and thin. It was our love that gave us the courage to persevere, to endure, and ultimately to emerge victorious.

Gratitude:

I am grateful to be here, alive and breathing, despite the misadventure we had. There were multiple moments during our time in Taroko when I was sure we wouldn't make it. Life is a precious gift, and I am filled with awe and appreciation for each new day.

I am grateful to our friends, family, and the brave rescue workers who stood by us during our darkest hours. Their love, support, and selflessness have been the foundation of our strength.

To the dedicated doctors and physiotherapists who worked to heal my body and restore my strength, I owe an immense debt of gratitude. Their expertise, compassion, and commitment to my recovery have been nothing short of miraculous, especially in getting me through the 'impossible mound.'

I am thankful for the support of my fitness trainers and yoga buddies, who have been invaluable sources of encouragement and inspiration on my journey to wellness. Their friendship and guidance have played a vital role in building my physical and emotional resilience.

To my employer and colleagues, I extend my deepest appreciation for their understanding and support during my time of need. Their generosity in providing mental health resources, medical insurance, and the necessary time to process the trauma before returning to work has been a lifeline during a challenging time.

My gratitude extends to my therapist and the meditation app, which have been indispensable tools for navigating the complexities of my inner landscape. Through therapy and mindfulness practices, I have gained invaluable insights and coping strategies for managing the aftermath of my ordeal. If you are looking for a recommendation for a meditation app, I use 'Waking Up.' They offer a 30-day free trial with a 28-day introductory programme, which got me hooked.

Finally, my heartfelt gratitude extends to the people of Taiwan, including the tourists, guests, and the remarkable staff of the Silks Place Hotel in Taroko National Park. Their kindness, hospitality, and solidarity touched my heart and reaffirmed my faith in the inherent goodness of humanity. A special shout-out to the spirit of global fellowship shown by the Rotary network for their swift and compassionate actions, particularly by PDG Young and PDG JP, who ensured our safety and well-being, providing us with a sense of belonging and family in a time of need.

In moments of hardship and adversity, it is easy to lose sight of the blessings that surround us. But through the practice of gratitude, we cultivate a deep sense of appreciation for the abundance of love, support, and grace that sustains us on our journey through life.

References

1. https://www.youtube.com/watch?v=ESLwcfNhYN8

2. https://www.youtube.com/watch?v=fsexKrdv3dU

3. https://www.instagram.com/stories/highlights/17975715872687689/

4. https://www.youtube.com/watch?v=dotg27TKQC0

5. https://www.youtube.com/watch?v=_A31FwHKAiA

6. https://www.youtube.com/watch?v=RlK-MSy1NO8

7. https://www.youtube.com/watch?v=jKhF0RPOhmU

8. https://www.hindustantimes.com/india-news/taiwan-earthquake-two-indians-missing-search-operations-underway-101712160076856.html

9. https://www.linkedin.com/posts/namrata-kohli_repost-taiwan-earthquake-activity-7182470166369243136-KJUH/

10. https://www.channelnewsasia.com/singapore/singapore-couple-taiwan-quake-survivors-trapped-taroko-national-park-4258026

Words of Love and Encouragement

You have navigated the turmoil you experienced with such depth. This book is exceptionally well written, and I couldn't be prouder of you. Your expression of each emotion is incredibly heartfelt. Gratitude shines through, and your humility and empathy are beautifully portrayed.

I wish you boundless success and will always pray for your safety and well-being. Embrace each day fully, without regrets. Approach relationships with love and patience, remembering not to judge, as everyone has their unique life journey and perspective.

Lots of love,
Ma

Each time I read this story, I am completely engrossed. Each chapter vividly brings to life what you went through, making me feel and imagine the harrowing experience you went through. This story provides readers with a rare insight into the sheer magnitude of an earthquake–something most people may never experience in their lifetime. The lessons of gratitude, love, and humanity learned in such a difficult time are truly profound.

Proud of you,
Papa

www.ingramcontent.com/pod-product-compliance
Lightning Source LLC
Chambersburg PA
CBHW031628170726
47990CB00017B/409